Story

of Ireland

Childcraft

Story of Ireland — a **Childcraft** title
Childcraft Reg. US Pat. Off. Marca Registrada

Copyright © 1988 by World Book, Inc.
World Book — Childcraft International
World Book House
77 Mount Ephraim
Tunbridge Wells
Kent TN4 8AZ, UK.

Printed in the USA.

ISBN 0 7166-6488-7

World Book — Childcraft International
Dollard House
Welling Quay
Dublin 2
Eire

Story
of Ireland

World Book, Inc.
a Scott Fetzer company
Chicago London Sydney
Toronto

Managing Editor: Felicia Law
Project Editor: Gerry Bailey
Authors: Gerry Bailey
                        Tim Wood
Designer: Felicia Law
Picture Research: Samantha Bentham

History Consultants: Professor Donnchadh O'Corrain
                        Dept of Irish History
                        University College, Cork.

                        Dr Anthony Stewart
                        Dept Modern History
                        The Queen's University of Belfast.

Educational Consultant: Seamus McDermott MA
                        Teacher of History, St. Malachy High School,
                        Castle Wellan

Contents

The first Irishmen

Two dark figures crouched low behind a wide tree trunk. Each carried a spear and a small flint axe. Suddenly, from the forest ahead of them, came a crashing, rustling sound. The hands of the two men tightened around the shafts of their spears. The crashing grew louder. Then into a nearby clearing lurched a huge, ugly boar.

Hunters like these lived in Ireland during the Mesolithic, or Middle Stone Age. They were tall, broad-shouldered people. Their foreheads were broad and high, their hair was brown and wavy, and their eyes were blue.

No one knows exactly when these people first came to Ireland, but it was probably around 9,000 years ago. They came to Britain through Europe. They reached Ireland by crossing the Irish Sea and the North Channel at the narrowest points. Their transport may have been either dug-out or skin-covered boats like the curraghs used by Donegal fishermen today. And because they made their tools and weapons out of stone, usually sharpened pieces of flint, they are called Stone Age people.

The people of the Middle Stone Age lived in Ireland for about 4,000 years. They were hunters. They hadn't learned to grow crops or herd animals. While some fished and hunted wild birds and animals for food, others gathered berries, roots and shellfish and made clothes from animal skins. They lived in huts, close to a source of water where they could also catch fish. And they knew how to make fire by rubbing pieces of flint together.

The farmers

The woman worked busily at the wooden loom. She was weaving wool into cloth, which she would use to make a tunic. Close by, a man chipped and scraped a piece of flint. Patiently he worked on the stone until he had a fine, sharp arrowhead. When he had finished, he placed the arrowhead with the others he had made. He only needed one for himself. The rest he would trade for meat or corn. Most of the people in the village were busy ploughing the nearby fields, getting ready to plant corn. Some hunted beasts in the forest, while others looked after a few sheep and cows.

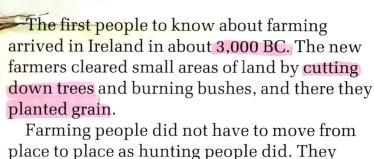

The first people to know about farming arrived in Ireland in about 3,000 BC. The new farmers cleared small areas of land by cutting down trees and burning bushes, and there they planted grain.

Farming people did not have to move from place to place as hunting people did. They settled in groups and built small villages. Their houses were made of wood and stone. To make a house they dug a shallow hole in the ground. Around this they built a frame of wooden poles. The frame was lined with skins on the inside, while sods of earth protected the outside. The roof was thatched with rushes. Inside the house were pottery jars for storing food and water. Because these farmers still used flint to make their tools, we call them Neolithic, or New Stone Age people.

Neolithic people buried their dead in stone tombs. The stones were very large, so the tombs were called megaliths, which means 'large stones'. They built two kinds of graves — court cairns and passage graves.

A passage grave is made up of stones piled in two lines which lead to a chamber also made of stones. A court cairn has an open area like a forecourt, leading to the burial chamber.

passage grave

A dolmen is a group of megaliths topped with a capstone.

Bronze!

The small boy drew near to the pit in which there glowed a fierce charcoal fire. He watched carefully as his uncle, the smith, threw pieces of metal into the flames.

As the charcoal glowed a brilliant red, the metal became hotter and hotter. Soon it began to melt and trickle down into the bottom of the pit. When all the metal had melted, the smith scraped aside the charcoal embers and scooped the soft metal into a stone pot, which he hung over a second fire. As the metal melted down again, the smith stirred hard. Finally the smith poured the liquid metal into a stone mould.

It was several hours before the metal cooled and the mould could be opened. The boy looked on as his uncle raised a perfectly-shaped bronze spearhead!

About 2,000 BC, people who knew how to make useful tools and weapons from a metal called bronze came to Ireland. Bronze is a mixture of copper and tin. These people had learned that if they heated gold, tin or copper to a high temperature, the metals would melt.

But tin or copper were too soft. So, somehow, these early people learned to make bronze. The time when people began to use bronze is called the Bronze Age.

Many of the Bronze Age people in Ireland were traders. They made ornaments of gold and bronze and traded them to visitors from Europe. Irish ornaments from the period have been found as far away as Spain and France.

Bronze was used to make weapons, tools and ornaments.

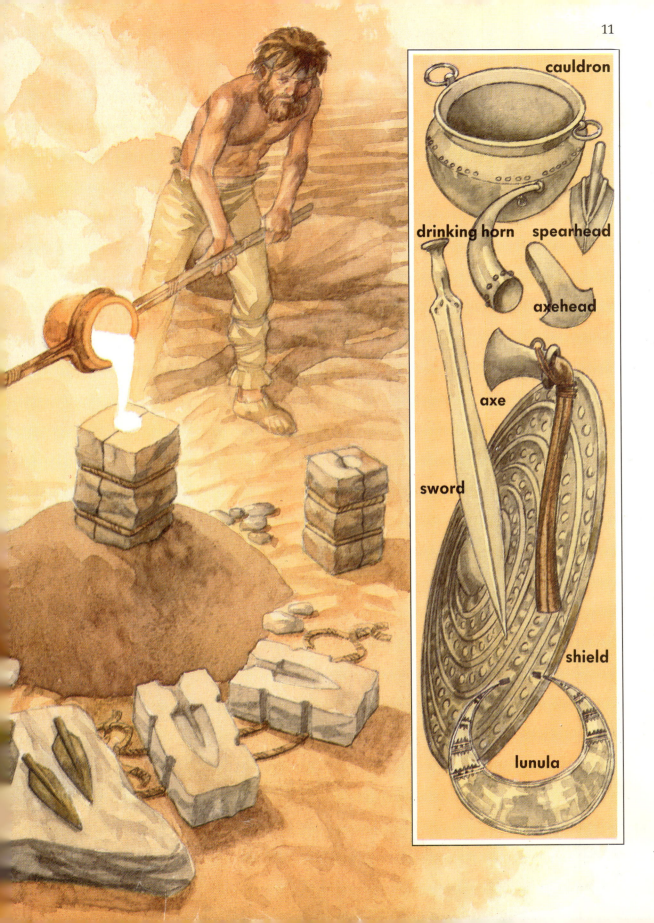

cauldron

drinking horn

spearhead

axehead

axe

sword

shield

lunula

The warriors

The two lookouts watched from their hiding place in the long grass. Coming towards them, along the shore, was a group of warriors. These fierce men were tall and blond, with blue eyes. They wore long moustaches and were dressed in brightly-coloured plaid tunics. Some wore beautifully-worked neck collars of bronze or gold. All carried sharp-edged swords of iron.

As soon as the warriors were well out of sight, the lookouts turned and fled. The warriors they had seen were Celts!

The first Celts came to Ireland in about 600 BC. They had spread slowly over land and sea from central Europe. Today, historians believe that the Celts came from an area east of the Rhine river and to the north of the Alps. Many years ago,

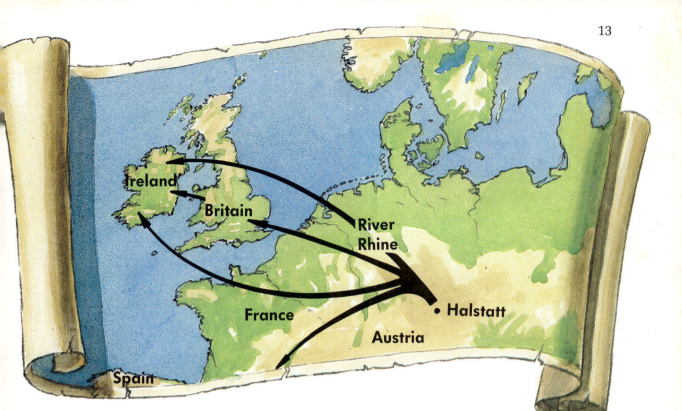

archaeologists unearthed a Celtic town in Hallstatt in Austria. There they found weapons and ornaments that were similar to those found in Ireland.

The Celts spread westwards into France, Spain and Britain, and then into Ireland.

Later, in about 250 BC, a second group of Celts began to move west across Europe, conquering new lands as they went. Within a hundred years, they too had reached Ireland. These fighting men were called La Tene Celts. They were fierce warriors who drove into battle in light chariots. They fought very bravely, without armour, and legends tell how they were not frightened of death.

The Celts ruled over Ireland, but many of the earlier Bronze Age peoples survived under their rule. Slowly, the Bronze Age customs changed to be more like those of the Celts.

In time Celtic ways and the Celtic language spread throughout Ireland. It has remained the language of Ireland down to modern times.

Cattle wealth

The farmer picked his way through the mud and straw. He had come to buy a new cow from his neighbour who had more cows than he needed. The farmer looked carefully at every cow, then picked out a fat one he liked. A deal was struck — a load of corn in exchange for the cow! The Celts in Ireland did not use money, but traded goods for other goods when they needed something. A person who owned a large number of animals was considered very wealthy.

Celtic farmers raised cattle, sheep and pigs. They grew wheat and oats for bread and porridge, and barley for beer-making. They also grew flax for making linen. Vegetables such as cabbage, onions and leeks were planted as well. The fields were tilled with simple iron-tipped ploughs which cut shallow grooves in the ground, although they did not turn the earth over as modern ploughs do.

Celtic farmers were often wealthy. Their clothes were woven from linen or wool and usually dyed in bright colours. They wore a type of long tunic called a 'leine'. Over this was slung a woollen cloak, kept in place by a brooch called a 'deilg'. Skilful metalsmiths forged these brooches, as well as neck collars called 'torcs' and other ornaments made from gold, silver and bronze.

Poets and kings

The stern-faced poet stood in front of the seated men. He raised both hands in the air. Then he spoke the last words of a long and spell-binding poem. The king looked satisfied. The lords who sat around him also nodded their approval. The poet had pleased them and he would be rewarded well for his work.

The poets of Celtic Ireland were called 'filid', and held a very special place of honour. Their training was long and hard. They had to

Raths were forts built of wood. A ditch was dug around the wooden wall and the earth piled up to make a bank called a rampart. Across the ditch lay a drawbridge which could be pulled up at night.

learn thousands of lines of verse. In their
poems they had to praise their king or lord,
and recall every detail of his past and the
history of his people. They also had to know
about the Celtic gods such as Danu, the mother
goddess, and Dagda, the father of the gods.
In fact, the filid were priests as well as poets.
Their poetry was thought to have great powers.
A strong, moving poem might cause the gods
to bring great success or great harm to its
audience.

A tribe was called a 'tuath'. The nobles of
the tribe chose their strongest lord or warrior
to be 'ri', or king. Sometimes one king would
become very powerful, and neighbouring
kings would have to show loyalty to him.
A powerful man like that was known as 'ard ri',
or high king.

Kings, nobles and farmers lived in circular
forts called 'raths'. These were surrounded by
high protective banks of earth. Legends tell
how the high kings of Ireland made their home
in the great rath of Tara. Many raths, like the
famous one of Tara, can still be seen today.

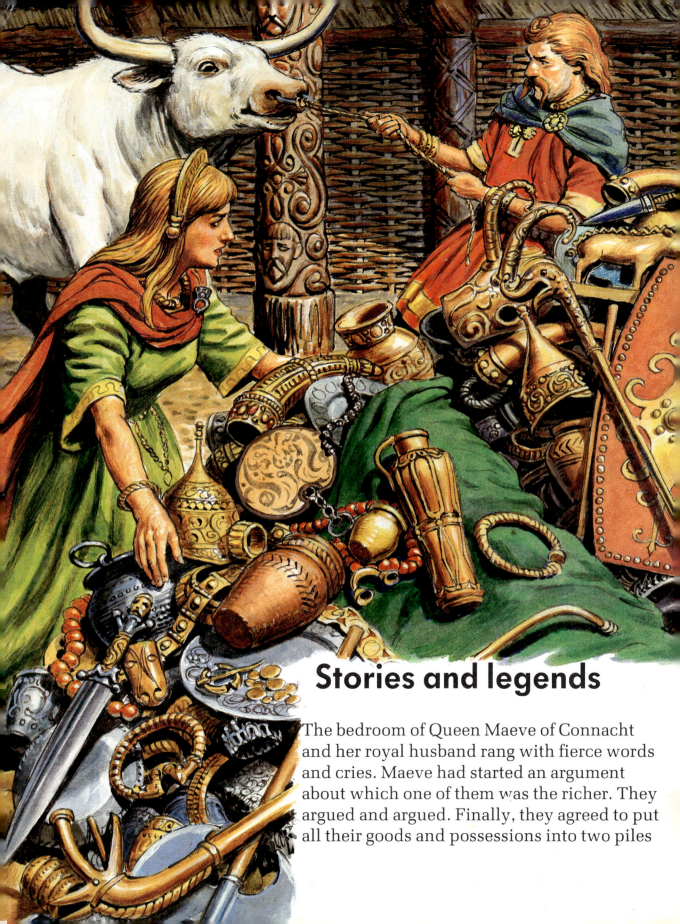

Stories and legends

The bedroom of Queen Maeve of Connacht and her royal husband rang with fierce words and cries. Maeve had started an argument about which one of them was the richer. They argued and argued. Finally, they agreed to put all their goods and possessions into two piles and compare them. It turned out that in almost every way they were equal, except for the great white bull that belonged to the king. The king had won the contest. Maeve was furious. She was determined to get a bull for herself, as fine as that of the king. The only one she knew of was the great brown bull of Cooley. And she resolved to have it.

This is how the legend of The Cattle-raid of Cooley, or the 'Tain Bo Cuailgne', begins. It is one of many legends written down between AD 600 and AD 1200.

All the stories are very old. They were first told by the poets, and passed on by word of mouth. Others were written down by learned men and their readers may have thought of them as accounts of real events. But they weren't. They were wonderful works of fantasy that, today, tell us something about how the Irish Celts lived. Through their characters, these tales describe how the Celts fought, feasted and played, and how they believed in gods and spirits of good or evil. Tales of Cúchulain, the boy warrior, of Finn mac Cool and the other heroes were the beginnings of Ireland's marvellous tradition of literature, folk-lore and legend.

The stories are told in four groups called cycles. The Myth Cycle tells about the first people to come to Ireland. It describes the deeds of gods, goddesses and heroes.

The Ulster Cycle tells about Conchobhar mac Nessa, king of Ulster, and the Red Branch Knights who made up his warrior band. The Cattle-raid of Cooley is the most important story in this cycle.

The last cycle is the King Cycle. This group of stories tells of the great kings of Ireland.

The Fenian Cycle tells the story of the 'Fianna', a band of heroic warriors that protected Ireland from evil. Its most famous leader was Finn mac Cool.

Cattle-raid of Cooley

The brown bull of Cooley belonged to an Ulsterman who, at first, was willing to lend his bull to Queen Maeve. But then he learned that she wanted the bull so much, she would have stolen it anyway. This made the Ulsterman shake with anger. And he decided that Maeve wouldn't have his bull, even if she paid him all the money in Connacht.

So Maeve gathered an army of brave Connachtmen, and went to capture the brown bull. It so happened that at this particular time each year, the Red Branch Knights of Ulster fell under a terrible spell. The spell made wise men foolish and strong men weak. Then it made all men fall into a deep sleep for a week.

Queen Maeve knew there would be no one awake to stop her and her army, so she marched north.

But the boy warrior, Cúchulain, was not bewitched by this spell for he was related to

the gods. When he heard that Maeve's army had reached the borders of Ulster, Cúchulain sent his charioteer to wake the Red Branch Knights. Meanwhile, he prepared to face the army alone.

Cúchulain ambushed the Connachtmen as they reached the Gap of the North. He picked them off with the stones from his sling. He even shot Maeve's pet raven which perched on her shoulder. Then he fought Maeve's champions one by one, and one by one he defeated them.

The Red Branch Knights awoke from their sleep at the sound of the alarm, but it was too late. Despite Cúchulain's bravery, a band of Connachtmen entered Ulster by trickery, and stole the brown bull.

When the brown bull reached Connacht it angered the white bull of the king, the two mighty animals locked horns in battle. Finally, the brown bull of Cooley was victorious. It set off to walk back to Ulster. But died of its wounds.

From that time on, the Ulstermen have told the story of the bull and how, Cúchulain held off the army of Connacht.

The Salmon of Knowledge

In the world of Celtic legend, there were two kinds of warriors. The first were the warriors of great tribes. Cúchulain was a tribal warrior and so were the Red Branch Knights. The second type of warriors had no tribe. They lived by their own laws and their own mighty deeds. They were known as the Fianna or Fenians. And their bravest leader was the son of Cool, the mighty Finn mac Cool.

This is one of the tales of Finn.

Once a boy was born who was given the name Demne by his mother. But later, because he grew so tall and blond, he was nick-named Finn, 'the fair one'.

Even as a young boy, Demne was very skilful. He was an expert hunter with the sling. No one could beat him at the game of hurling. And he was a master of single combat, the sport of fighting man against man. The only things he had still to gain were the art of poetry and the gift of wisdom.

One day, Demne was sent to study with the old poet, Finneces. Finneces lived on the broad banks of the River Boyne. For seven years he had lived alone beside a pool, where, it was said, the sacred Salmon of Knowledge lived. Now Finneces knew very well that it had been prophesied that a man by the name of Finn would catch and eat the fish. But the old poet thought long and hard. Why shouldn't he, Finneces, eat the fish instead and possess all the wisdom of the world? After all, his name sounded very much like the Finn of the prophecy. So Finneces set to work, and at last he managed to catch the sacred fish. Quickly he ordered his pupil, Demne, to cook it. But he warned that on no account was Demne to taste even so much as a morsel of its flesh.

Demne did as he was told and brought the great salmon to his master.

"Have you eaten any of it?" scowled Finneces.

"No," replied Demne. "But I burned my thumb on it and had to suck the burn to stop the pain."

"What is your name?" begged the old poet.

"Demne."

"And is that your only name?"

"Well, some people call me Finn," replied the boy.

"Then eat the salmon, Finn," sighed the poet. "For it is yours by right."

So Finn ate the salmon and gained all the knowledge of the world. And ever afterwards, whenever he put his thumb in his mouth, he could foresee the future.

Now he was brave and skilful - and wise!

The lands of Conn and Mugg

The two great kings leaned on their long swords and gazed into the distance. Their eyes followed the low ridge of hills that marked the

horizon. The ridge was called Escir Riada.

It snaked across Ireland from Dublin Bay in the east, to Galway Bay in the west. This, the kings agreed, was to be the division. North of the ridge would be Conn's half. South of the ridge would be Mugg's half.

The story of how the country came to be divided into two halves comes from the King Cycle. No one knows exactly what happened, but it's possible that a powerful king in the north of Ireland gathered several other kings around him and became their leader. According to the story, the name of this king was Conn of the Hundred Battles of Connacht. That is why the north was called Conn's half. And the great rath of Tara became its capital.

In the south, another group of kings banded together. Their centre was at Cashel, now in County Tipperary. The leaders of this group were all descended from a great warrior, Mugg Nuadat, who was also called Eogan. They called themselves Eoganachta or descendants of Eogan. Their half of the land was called Mugg's half.

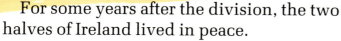

For some years after the division, the two halves of Ireland lived in peace.

Before the division of Ireland into two halves, the old stories tell how the country was divided into five parts, or fifths.

To the north was Ulaid, or Ulster; to the east was Laigin, which is Leinster; to the west Connacht; and to the south Mumu, or Munster.

The fifth part was called Mide, which means middle. Mide may have been a small area around what we now call County Meath. But some people think it was not really an area at all, just the name for a point where the four great kingdoms met.

The names of four of the fifths of Ireland are still in use today as names of the provinces of Ireland.

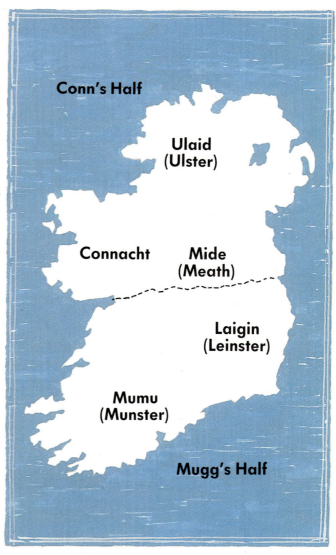

Conn's Half

Ulaid
(Ulster)

Connacht   Mide
(Meath)

Laigin
(Leinster)

Mumu
(Munster)

Mugg's Half

The Ui Neill

It had been a great battle. The people of the north had resisted Niall's army to the end, but at last they had accepted defeat. Now they stood before their new conqueror, feeling tired and depressed. Standing in his chariot, Niall towered above them all.

"Let the strongest and tallest of you stand forward," he declared. "There will be no more bloodshed today, but your best warriors will be bound and led to my camp. There they will be held hostage. They will be safe, providing you all accept me as your king."

Niall was now the greatest king of the people of Conn, the people descended from Conn of the Hundred Battles. In all, Niall conquered and ruled over nine smaller kingdoms. To keep the peace in his great territory, he took hostages from every defeated kingdom. He became known as Niall of the Nine Hostages.

Niall was a great leader. He managed to unite much of Ireland in the north. He also led

his Irish armies in daring raids against the Romans in Britain.

The descendants of Niall of the Nine Hostages were known as the Ui Neill. They ruled over a large part of Ireland for many years after Niall's death. Their centre was Tara. They held a feast at Tara each time a new king came to power. The Fair of Tailtiu was held close by. Here the lords came to talk about political matters, to enjoy entertainments, games and contests and to watch horse-racing.

Hundreds of years later, a descendant of the Ui Neill, called Niall Glundubh, began the great family that was to become the O'Neills of Tyrone. Today, many people all over the world are proud to be called O'Neill.

Saint Patrick

Just an arm's length away stood a huge, panting figure whose shadow blocked out all the light. After a long chase, the youth was cornered. He shook with fear. The figure gripped the youth in his strong arms and carried him outside. Here, the frightened youth was thrown down beside other captives from his town. He was not going to die after all. He was to live as a slave to the pagan Irish!

The boy's name was Patrick, and he had grown up in a wealthy Christian family in Britain. Now he was to be shipped to Ireland, where he would work as a shepherd for six long years. But Patrick was clever and one day he escaped.

Patrick was no longer the youth taken in the raid so long ago. Something had happened to him during his years in the hills and

mountains. He felt that God was close to him.

Leaving Ireland, Patrick made his way home to Britain. There he studied religion and became a Christian bishop. His dearest wish was to convert the pagan Irish, and he felt he heard their voices asking him to come back. Imagine how Patrick felt when he learned that he would be able to return to Ireland! But now, as a bishop, he would preach to the people of Ulaid.

It is likely that there were some Christians in Ulaid already. Patrick must have been pleased by this, but perhaps he knew there was a greater challenge ahead. For when his mission was doing well, he left and went to work among the people of the west coast. These people were pagans. They did not believe in a Christian God, but in the gods and goddesses of legend and myth.

Patrick was a very successful missionary, although his travels were often dangerous. Many people were converted to Christianity by him.

Today, Saint Patrick is remembered as the patron saint of Ireland.

Sacred study

The young monk solemnly placed another thin sheet of fine leather, called vellum, on the table where he sat. In one corner of his cell glowed the weak flame of a half-used candle. It was getting late and night was closing in. But the monk did not notice the fading light. He took up his pen and began to write in beautiful, rounded letters. His writing and his learning were more important to him than anything else. For like all the students at the monastery of Clonard, sacred study was his way of showing his love of God.

In Patrick's times, just as today, not all of the men called to God wanted to join the church as priests or bishops. Some wanted to study the scriptures and worship in a simpler way. They sometimes formed groups, or communities. The place where they lived was called a monastery and they were called monks. Irish monks often worked as missionaries, travelling around to teach people about Christianity, just as Patrick had done.

After Patrick's death, the monasteries became the most important religious centres in Ireland. And there were many of them. Saint Finnian's monastery at Clonard was one. Other famous monasteries were built at Durrow, Clonfert, Clonmacnoise and Bangor. They were often founded in lonely places, like Skellig — a rocky and barren island off the south-west coast.

A monk's life was hard. He had to obey his superiors without question. Often he fasted, or went without food. And punishments for sinful thoughts or deeds were severe.

Irish monks spent much time writing and copying books and manuscripts. The monks were the first people to write down the old Irish sagas and legends. The Irish had a written language called 'ogham'. But the ogham alphabet was made up of groups of lines which were carved into tall stones. This language could not be used to create books. The monks wrote in Latin, the language of the Church of Rome. Later they wrote in Gaelic, the language of the Celts. In their cold, gloomy cells, they created the first written literature of Ireland.

The famous Ogham Stone still stands at Kilmakedar. It is carved with ogham writing.

The Dove of the Church

Tiny waves crept along the shore as the small boat pulled out to sea. A few people watched the boat and waved. No one said a word. Perhaps some cried. In the boat Columcille and his twelve companions turned their backs on Ireland and set off towards the island of Iona, off the west coast of Scotland.

Columcille was a member of the great Ui Neill family. In fact three of his cousins were Ui Neill kings. Columcille himself was a poet. He knew much about the old Irish learning, but he was also a faithful Christian. He had studied hard to become a learned monk. And at the beginning of his career he had even started famous monasteries at Durrow and Derry. What happened next we do not know for sure.

It is said that Columcille went to visit Saint Finnian, and that while he was there he copied one of Saint Finnian's books. His host was very upset. He asked the high king to judge whether Columcille had done the right thing. The king said "To every cow her calf, to every book its copy". He was saying that only the person who owns a book should copy it. Columcille was angered by this. He gathered together an army, supported by several of his loyal relations, to fight against the king. But when the fighting had finished, Columcille was full of sorrow at the trouble he had caused. He decided to leave Ireland and save as many souls as had been lost in the battle.

Whatever the reason, Columcille sailed to the island of Iona in about AD 563. He was

Iona Abbey stands on the spot where Saint Columba founded his famous monastery.

given permission to found a monastery there by the king of the Picts, whose lands lay to the north of the island. Soon, the monastery at Iona became one of the best-known centres of learning and study in the west of Europe.

Columcille worked for over thirty years among the Picts, Gaelic-speaking Scots and Britons. His Gaelic learning helped him understand these peoples, and how best to teach them Christianity. Columcille died in about AD 597 and was buried on Iona. We remember him today as Saint Columba, the Dove of the Church.

The picture below shows how Saint Columba's monastery might have looked.

The Golden Age

Many Irish monks followed in Columcille's footsteps. They travelled far and wide, establishing monasteries and schools. One such monk, Columbanus, is famous for the monasteries he started in Europe, such as Luxeuil in France and Bobbio in Italy. In time, Irish learning and art became known as the most brilliant in the Christian world. Irish teachers were welcomed to royal courts and places of learning all over Europe.

It was during this time that the beautiful illuminated, or decorated, manuscripts were created. These were works of art as well as

A page from the Book of Kells, worked in illuminated manuscript.

learning. But there were other marvellous creations as well. We call this wonderful period, between AD 600 and AD 900, the Golden Age of Ireland.

The Book of Kells is said to be the most beautiful of all the illuminated manuscripts. Some say that it was written by Columcille's monks in Iona, many years after his death. It was preserved for centuries at the monastery of Kells in what is now County Meath. Many different monks probably worked on it. Some may have been good at certain types of pictures, others at designs and others at drawing people and animals.

Irish Christians created magnificent, tall crosses. They were put up to mark the boundary of a monastery, and also as monuments to God.

The Ardagh chalice is made of bronze, silver and gold. It was probably used at a great monastery. It was made in the eighth century.

The Tara Brooch is decorated with swirls, patterns and tiny animals, just like the pictures in the manuscripts. This is one of the most treasured pieces of Celtic art that can be seen today.

People of the longboats

Through fine morning mist, the old abbot made out the hazy outline of a ship's prow. He listened carefully and heard the faint splash, splash of oars dipping into the water. Soon a great, square sail came into view. The abbot's heart pounded. It was a longboat. The Vikings were coming!

Quickly, the old man climbed the hill that led to the monastery. He sounded the alarm bell and monks began to gather before him. Some had been at prayer, some preparing the morning meal and others had been at work in the library. The monks collected what they could – books, candlesticks, and a few sacred objects.

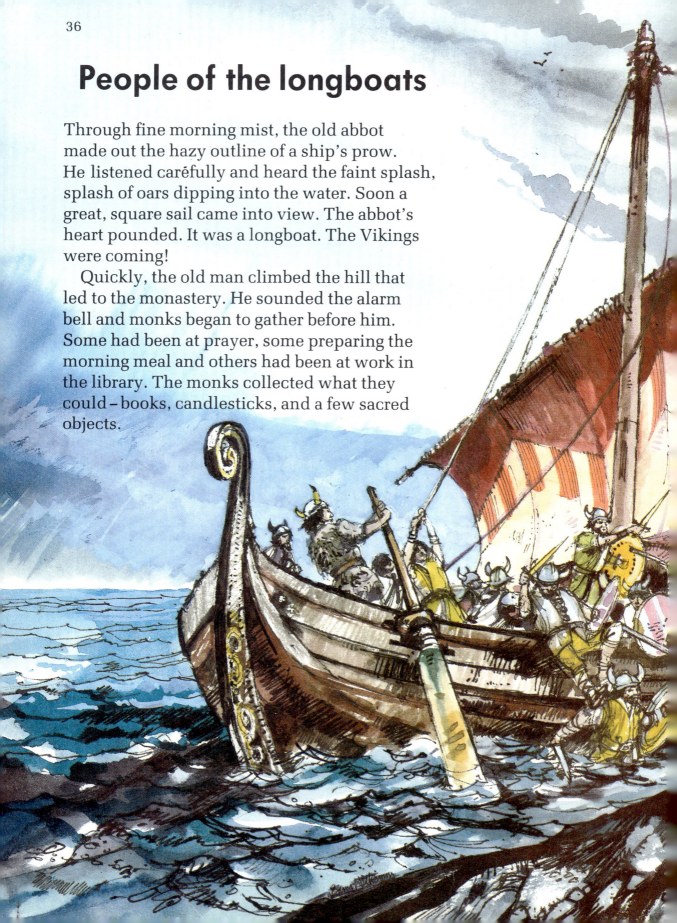

But it was too late. The echoing yells of the Vikings grew louder. Some of the monks knelt to pray. Others looked for somewhere to run. The old abbot gazed sorrowfully at his people. Then the Vikings were upon them. They were a terrifying sight with their helmets and sharp swords. They cut down the monks who would not flee. They burned the buildings. And they stole all the gold and silver they could find. When the raid was over, they returned to their longboat and set off back to their settlement further up the Irish coast.

Raids like this one were frequent. The Vikings had come originally from Norway in Scandinavia. They were great sailors as well as master shipbuilders. They had left their homeland because the land was poor and their population was growing. They needed to find a new land to settle in. They also sailed for another reason, to enjoy the adventure and to steal booty. They raided all over Europe, including the coasts of Britain and Ireland. Mostly they attacked the wealthy churches and monasteries. The first record of a Viking attack in Ireland was in AD 795. Soon they had built settlements along the east and south coasts.

Brian of the Tributes

The story of Brian of the Tributes begins when the Vikings first arrived in Ireland in the ninth century and started to take control of the country. Many kingdoms in the south fell easily into the invaders' hands, but one small kingdom resisted. This was Dal Cais, which was led by Mathgamain and his brother Brian.

The armies of Dal Cais were strong, and eager to conquer other kingdoms. Soon they were successful in challenging the Vikings in their newly-won territories, and the power of all the main Celtic families in the south. Even after Mathgamain was killed, Brian continued his victorious campaign. One after another, the southern kingdoms came under his control. Because they all paid taxes, or tributes, to Brian, he became known as Brian of the Tributes.

Not content with his great southern kingdom, Brian rode north. The northern kings were stubborn and strong, but even they gave into him. In the year AD 1002, Brian became king of Tara. Now he was king of almost all of Ireland. But Brian ruled by force, and by the strength of his personality. When he was not around, arguments broke out. The men of Leinster particularly hated being under his rule. In 1014 they asked the Vikings of Dublin and friendly armies from overseas to join them in an uprising.

The two armies met on April 23rd 1014 at Clontarf near Dublin, and a great battle took place. Brian's army won in the end, but a sad event spoiled their victory. Some escaping Leinstermen, led by Brodor of Man, accidentally found themselves outside Brian's tent. They overcame his surprised bodyguards and entered the tent. Inside they killed the famous leader.

The Vikings never again made war on the Celtic Irish, but nothing would stop the Celtic kings from quarrelling amongst themselves.

The town-makers

The waterfront bustled with excitement and activity. Two foreign boats had just arrived. One had come from Gaul, which is now France. It brought many flagons of rich wine. The other had come from further east. It carried spices, precious stones and other fine goods. The Viking merchants had fine weapons, ornaments and woollens to trade for these rich cargoes. The two ships would leave, full of Irish goods to be sold in faraway ports.

The Vikings, who called themselves Ostmen, are famous in history for their fierce fighting and their plundering. But they were also skilled traders and businessmen. They built towns near the sea or at the mouths of wide rivers where they could carry out their trading. The most important trading town in

Ireland was the Ostman town of Dublin at the mouth of the river Liffey. The town was surrounded by a wooden wall. It had streets paved with wood, as well as wooden buildings and workshops. Dublin soon became a centre for trade on the east coast of Ireland. Coins were minted at Dublin. They looked the same as English silver coins, because they were used mainly to trade with the English.

Trade with other countries flourished. But later on, metal goods were manufactured and sold at home. By the year AD 1000, Viking designs were being copied in places like Clonmacnoise, on the river Shannon, which had become a centre for Irish crafts.

Although the first Ostmen worshipped their own gods such as Thor and Odin, most of the citizens of Dublin were Christians. And by the time of the Battle of Clontarf in 1014, Dublin had its own churches.

Swordland

After the Battle of Clontarf, Ireland was divided into main kingdoms and small sub-kingdoms. The kingdoms seemed always to be at war with one another. Sometimes they fought over land or cattle, and sometimes they fought over who was to be the high king, the king of all Ireland. Whoever was stronger at the time would call himself high king. But no one was ever strong enough to unite the whole country.

Connacht was ruled by the O'Connors. They had two capitals, one at Tuam and one at Galway. They built large castles at these places to protect themselves. Brefne was ruled by the O'Rourkes. It was a sub-kingdom of Connacht.

Munster was the most powerful kingdom in the south. It was ruled by the O'Briens, the descendants of Brian Boru. Their headquarters were at Kincora.

The MacCarthys, whose ancestors were the old Eoganacht kings, were rivals of the O'Briens. Sometimes they defeated the O'Briens and became kings of Munster instead.

Connacht

Tuam

Galway

Limerick

Munster

Cork

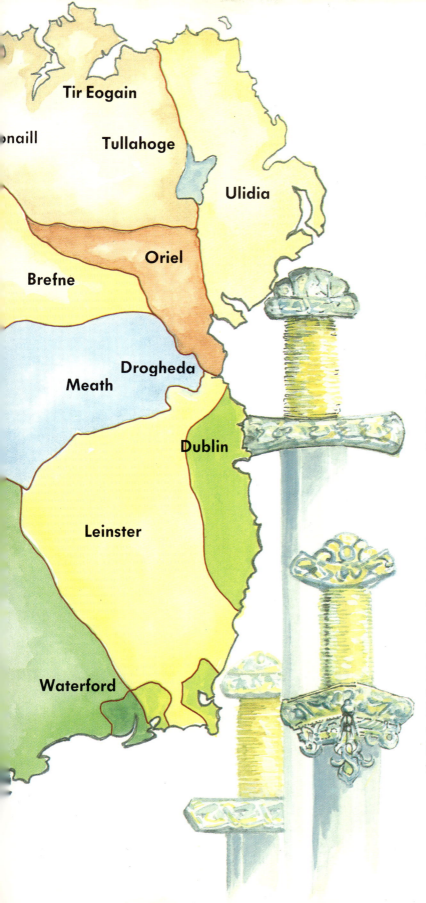

In the north, Tír Eogain was the most powerful kingdom. The kings of Tír Eogain lived at Tullahoge, near Lough Neagh. Three sub-kingdoms surrounded Tír Eogain. They were Tír Conaill, Ulidia and Oriel. They were supposed to be loyal to the Tír Eogain kings but they often fought against them.

The kingdom of Meath had little power after the death of its great king, Malachy II. It was constantly being conquered by the other kingdoms and its land divided between them.

The kingdom of Leinster was ruled by the MacMurrough family. Dermot I declared himself king in 1042. He made war on Munster and Meath, and defeated the king of Connacht. While Dermot was king, Leinster was the most powerful kingdom in Ireland. But when he was killed in battle, the kingdom was weakened. It soon became the weakest of all the great kingdoms.

The Normans

The small group of armoured knights waited on horseback on the crest of the low hill. Before them, in line, were seventy archers. The knights' leader, Strongbow, calmly watched as the Irish soldiers began to run uphill towards them. Then, at the moment when the Irish raised their whirling slings above their heads to release their stones, Strongbow stood upright in his stirrups and waved an arm.

At this signal, the Norman archers drew their bows and loosed their arrows. The shafts rained down on the Irish. Without armour, they were defenceless. They fell in their hundreds, dead or wounded. Then Strongbow blew his horn and the Norman knights charged down the hill. The Irish fought bravely, but within a few minutes the Normans had won. The road to Dublin was clear, and within a few days, the city would be theirs.

For many years, the Irish kings had been fighting each other to decide which of them should be the high king. One of them, Dermot MacMurrough, king of Leinster, had crossed to Wales for help. There, he had found supporters among the Norman lords. One, the Earl of Pembroke, known as Strongbow, brought an army of armoured knights and skilled archers to Ireland. They proved too much for the badly trained and poorly armoured Irish soldiers.

After capturing Dublin, the Normans did not return home. Strongbow married Eva, Dermot MacMurrough's daughter. Then, when Dermot died, Strongbow made himself king of Leinster. His Norman army stayed on. His knights conquered much of Ireland and built castles to defend their newly-won lands.

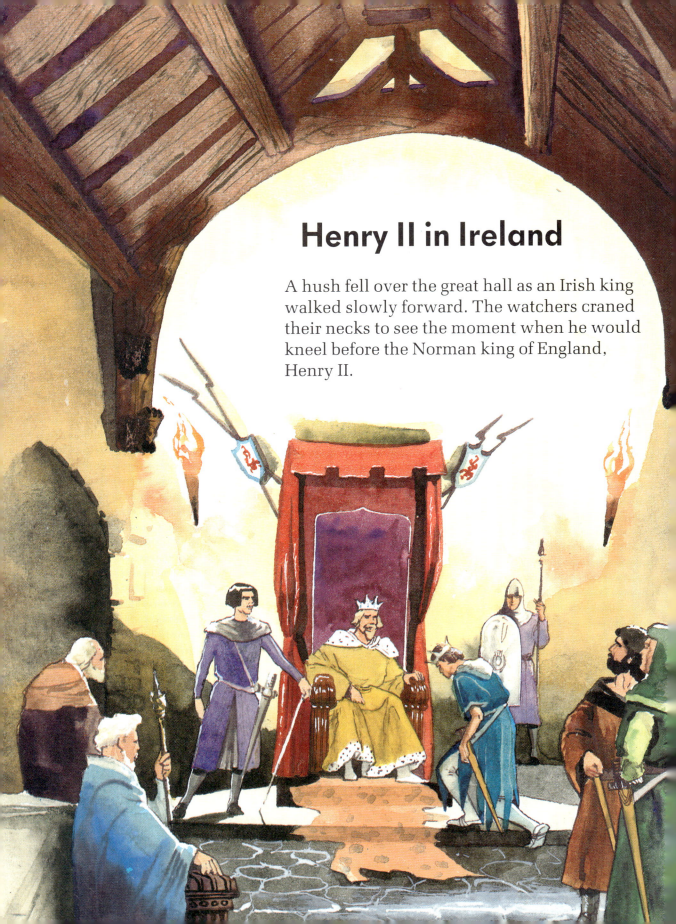

Henry II in Ireland

A hush fell over the great hall as an Irish king walked slowly forward. The watchers craned their necks to see the moment when he would kneel before the Norman king of England, Henry II.

Proudly he approached the throne and bent down. He kissed the ring on Henry's finger, and spoke. His words rang clear and true so that everyone present could hear them. He accepted Henry as his master, as Lord of Ireland.

This was the scene in 1171 as the Irish kings swore loyalty to Henry II, king of England. They wanted Henry to protect them from the Norman lords and their great armies, who were conquering their kingdoms.

Although Henry had allowed these Norman barons to go to Ireland in the first place, and although they were his friends and allies, he agreed to protect the Irish kings from them. Henry could see that the barons were becoming more and more powerful. He was worried that they could become as powerful as himself.

The solution was simple. The Irish kings swore their loyalty to Henry. When this was done, Henry became their overlord. From now on, anyone who attacked them would become the English king's enemy.

Henry had great hopes for his clever plan. But the Norman kings who followed Henry found that it did not bring peace to the land.

The Justiciar was the king of England's representative in Ireland, but had little real power. He was advised by the tenants-in-chief, but they rarely did what he told them.

The feudal system

From 1066 onwards, England, and later also Ireland, was ruled by Norman kings. The Normans brought their servants and armies of knights with them. They also brought a system of ruling the land — the feudal system.

The king of England owned all the land in Ireland, but he rarely visited the country. He rewarded his most loyal barons with gifts of Irish land.

They became tenants-in-chief of the king's land. Some of them owned whole kingdoms. They often fought each other, hoping to win even more land. They collected taxes from their sub-tenants, so many became very rich.

The sub-tenants were Norman knights. They fought for one Norman baron and swore to help him. In return they were given land. They built castles and controlled the peasants who lived on their land.

The peasants were allowed to work on the land and keep some of what they grew. The rest was given to their lord. They had few rights and were not always treated well by their Norman overlords.

50

The first Irish Parliament

"And so, my lords, the fighting must stop!"

John de Wogan looked round sternly at the assembled nobles. The great lords of nine counties and the other barons nodded reluctantly.

"Yes," thought de Wogan. "You all want peace but you also hate each other. I must be strong enough to control you all."

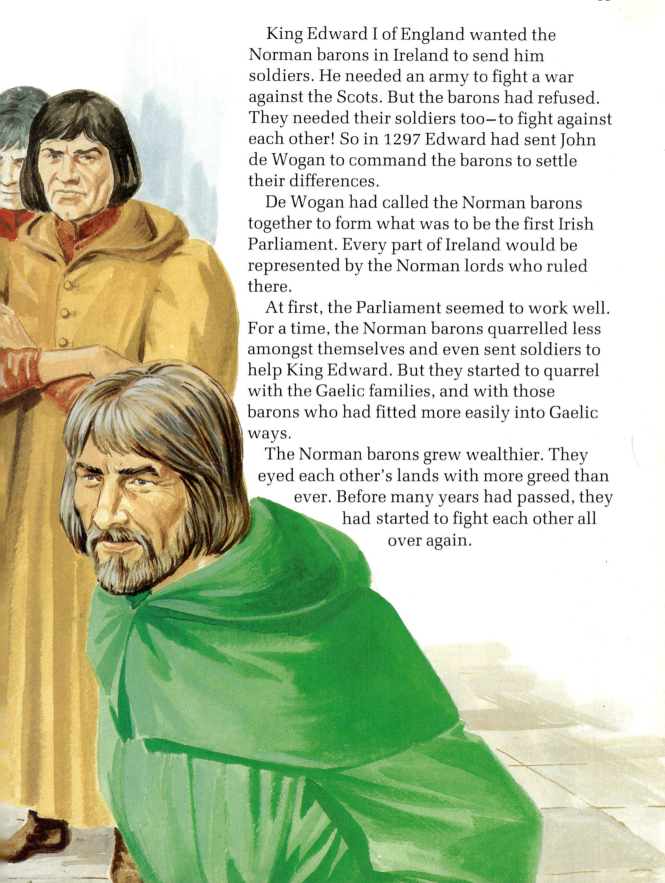

King Edward I of England wanted the Norman barons in Ireland to send him soldiers. He needed an army to fight a war against the Scots. But the barons had refused. They needed their soldiers too—to fight against each other! So in 1297 Edward had sent John de Wogan to command the barons to settle their differences.

De Wogan had called the Norman barons together to form what was to be the first Irish Parliament. Every part of Ireland would be represented by the Norman lords who ruled there.

At first, the Parliament seemed to work well. For a time, the Norman barons quarrelled less amongst themselves and even sent soldiers to help King Edward. But they started to quarrel with the Gaelic families, and with those barons who had fitted more easily into Gaelic ways.

The Norman barons grew wealthier. They eyed each other's lands with more greed than ever. Before many years had passed, they had started to fight each other all over again.

The Gallowglasses

Sir Guy's Norman knights looked around nervously as they rode deeper into the forest. They fingered the hilts of their swords and urged their horses into a trot. This was the sort of place for an ambush!

Suddenly there was a great shout. From among the trees poured a mass of soldiers wearing chain mail. They rushed at the Norman horsemen, swinging their great axes. The Norman column was split, and the knights scattered. A few managed to escape, but the axemen made short work of the rest.

The axemen were called Gallowglasses. This strange word came from the Gaelic words that described foreign soldiers, 'gall-oglaigh'. These soldiers were mostly Scots from the Hebrides, islands off the north-west coast of Scotland. They had been hired by the Gaelic Irish kings to fight against the Norman lords. The Gallowglasses were tough and skilful. They won many victories over the Normans.

By 1300, the Normans were no longer as powerful as they had been a hundred years before. Their armies were weakened from constant wars. Sometimes they fought the Irish, but mostly they fought each other, greedily trying to snatch more land for themselves.

The destroyer of Ireland

On June 24th 1314, a great battle was fought at Bannockburn in Scotland. The king of the Scots was called Robert Bruce. He was a powerful leader and his victory drove the English out of Scotland. But the English had not heard the last of the Bruce family, for Robert had a brother called Edward.

Edward Bruce was Earl of Carrick in Galloway, in Northern Scotland. Edward decided to make war on the English in Ireland, and become the hero of the Irish just as his brother had been for the Scots. After all, both countries were similar, containing peoples who were a mixture of Gaelic-speakers, Normans and English.

So in 1315, Edward Bruce landed in Ireland with an army of 6,000 Scottish soldiers. Soon he was defeating the small armies of the Norman lords, and attacking town after town, killing, burning and stealing as he went. It looked as if nothing would stop Edward Bruce from conquering all Ireland.

But one town decided to try. The great fortress of Carrickfergus Castle had become a refuge for many of the defeated Norman soldiers. Edward knew he must capture Carrickfergus, but he found the castle gates closed and barricaded. For many months Edward Bruce besieged the castle, hurling rocks at its walls. Inside, the people were starving. No food could get through, so the soldiers chewed on animal hides to try to keep themselves alive. At last they surrendered and, with this long-awaited victory, Edward crowned himself king of Ireland.

But the siege had not been in vain. The citizens of Dublin had taken heart from the brave resistance of Carrickfergus Castle. They too defended their city, building up its walls and destroying important bridges and roadways.

Edward Bruce never conquered Dublin, and the two long sieges gave the English king time to send new, strong armies to defend Ireland.

The Black Death

Friar Clyn sighed deeply and put down his quill. The words he was writing made him feel sad and weary. But he knew that he must go on. For Friar Clyn was describing the horrors of a great plague, which people were calling the Black Death.

Later, he wrote that if he should die of the plague too, he would leave parchment and ink ready for someone else to carry on. Secretly he believed that no one would escape the plague.

And sadly, shortly after this entry, Friar Clyn's story ends. In another person's handwriting is written, 'it appears that the author died here'. As the Friar had foretold, he did not live to finish his work.

The Black Death began in Europe. It spread into Ireland in the winter of 1348-49. The plague was a sickness spread by fleas that lived on black rats. No one knew how to cure it.

Friar Clyn tells us that it was rare for only one person to die in a household. Usually, the husband, wife, children and servants all died. The worst-hit places were the cities, where people lived closer together. Dublin and Drogheda lost almost all their population.

Friar Clyn died before he finished his story.

The plague was spread by fleas that lived on black rats.

The Norman settlers suffered badly. Many who lived in the east of Ireland fled from their manors into the cities. Soon they were fleeing back to England. The Gaelic Irish suffered less. Many lived in the countryside, where homes were spread out and the inhabitants less likely to catch the disease from each other. The plague killed many Norman settlers and the Gaelic Irish saw their opportunity. They began to move into lands which they had lost years before.

Victims of the plague were buried quickly.

The Statutes of Kilkenny

The young man threw the ball high into the air. Then he struck it a mighty blow with his hurling stick. Some of the watchers cheered, but others muttered among themselves. For the young men playing the game of hurling were not true Gaelic Irishmen, and by law they were not allowed to play this Irish game.

Although the players lived in Ireland, they were the sons of Norman or English settlers. They were 'English born in Ireland', and not from Irish Gaelic families, and came to be known as the Anglo-Irish. They lived in the Anglo-Irish part of Ireland in the south-east. This region was called the English Pale. The people of the Pale were loyal to the English king, and here the Viceroy or king's deputy, Lionel of Clarence, was obeyed.

But, in the year 1361, Clarence was worried. He had been told to make sure that the lands owned by the Anglo-Irish were never taken back by the Gaelic Irish. He had been told to

keep the two Irish peoples separate. Indeed,
the Anglo-Irish were forbidden to do anything
that might make them like the Gaelic Irish.
Clarence had made laws, or statutes, to make
sure this happened. They were called the
Statutes of Kilkenny, for it was in that city that
the Parliament met to pass them.

As well as not being allowed to play Irish
ball games, the Anglo-Irish were forbidden to
use light Irish saddles on their horses. They
might only use heavy Norman ones. They were
not allowed to speak the Gaelic language, only
English. They could not marry into Gaelic
families or wear Gaelic clothes. Neither could
they invite Gaelic minstrels, poets or
storytellers into their homes.

The statutes were full of severe laws like
this, and not surprisingly, few people paid
them any attention. The Anglo-Irish wanted to
share all the good things about Irish life, and
despite Lionel of Clarence, they continued to
do just what they wanted. They became just as
Irish as the Gaelic Irish themselves.

The Gaelic revival

The tall Norman knight smiled gently at his new Irish bride. Some years back, his ancestors had arrived in Ireland from their home in England. They had known little about their new country and its people. Now he had an Irish wife — a lady from a noble, land-owning family. Together they would command a large estate of land. Their children would grow up speaking Gaelic. The family would be truly Irish. Yes, he was looking forward to his new life as an Irishman!

He had other plans too. As a noble lord, he would be able to invite poets and scholars to live in his home. He might even write a little poetry in Gaelic himself. He looked forward to enjoying the company of such masters of

words and music. The knight had heard too, of
learned Gaelic historians, lawyers and doctors.
Through them he hoped to know more of
Gaelic traditions and customs. He might read
the great books and even order a scribe to make
a book for him like 'the Yellow Book of Lecan',
or 'Leabhor Breac'. This book told of the great
days of Tara and contained a picture of its
famous banqueting hall. And he would seek
out volumes like the Book of Ballymote, which
held many other tales.

Through his marriage and his love of
learning, the knight would soon lose his
Norman ways, and even forget much of his
English upbringing. In time he would become
as Irish as his wife. He was one of many
English Normans who were drawn to the
richness and strength of the Gaelic Irish
tradition.

The Great Earl

The young man sat well upon his horse. He stared boldly at the huge estate that lay before him. It was all his! And in time, he thought, it would become even bigger. The man's name was Garret More Fitzgerald and he was Earl of Kildare. One day he would become the most powerful man in all Ireland.

When his father died, Garret More was elected Viceroy, or king's deputy. He was chosen by the members of the Council of Ireland, which was part of the government. But the English king, Henry VII, did not agree with this choice. He tried to have Garret More removed from his position. But, in his own country, Garret More was too powerful, and King Henry had to give in. The Irishman continued as Viceroy. The Great Earl, as he came to be known, strengthened his position by forming friendships with other noble families.

By now, Garret More was more like a king than a king's deputy. Supported by friends, his army marched up and down the country, defeating his enemies. Garret More forced the people of the Pale to provide food and shelter for his troops. This order was called 'coign and livery' and most ordinary people did not like it.

Garret More continued to anger Henry VII by his actions in Ireland. But so powerful was the Great Earl that the king could not oppose him. Later, Henry said that "since all Ireland cannot rule this man, he shall rule all Ireland!" And so he did, until his death in 1513.

Silken Thomas

Bridles and swords jangled as the horsemen
rode into Dublin town. At the head of the band
rode Thomas Fitzgerald, Lord Offaly, the
eldest son of the Earl of Kildare. Each rider

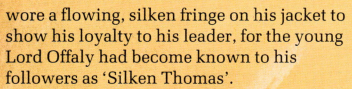

wore a flowing, silken fringe on his jacket to show his loyalty to his leader, for the young Lord Offaly had become known to his followers as 'Silken Thomas'.

Thomas was a proud young man. He had been left in charge of the Kildare family estates when his father was summoned to the court of the English king, Henry VIII. But Thomas had an even greater responsibility in his father's absence — he was also in charge of the government of Ireland.

The horsemen stopped outside the chamber of the ruling Council at St Mary's Abbey. Thomas stormed in and flung down the great Sword of State, the symbol of his authority. He told the astonished councillors that he would no longer serve as the king's representative in Ireland. He had heard that his father had been executed in the Tower of London. Now he was the king's enemy!

Thomas was promised support by the Pope in Italy, for the Pope had quarrelled with the English king. Thomas quickly took control of most of Leinster and the Pale, and marched to Dublin. But the Pope's troops did not arrive in time to help. Thomas was easily defeated by the English army, who had new cannons and guns. Thomas surrendered and was taken as prisoner to the Tower of London. In his cell in the Beauchamp Tower, Silken Thomas scratched his name into the stone wall. 'Thomas FitzG' can still be seen carved there. Perhaps there was no time to finish the name, for in 1537, Thomas and five of his uncles were beheaded.

The Book of Common Prayer

The old clergyman stood solemnly before his small congregation. Slowly, he opened the prayer book in his hand. Then, just as slowly, he began to read. At the end of the prayer, everyone said "Amen", although some Gaelic Irish had not understood a single word the priest had said. For the prayer book he had used was the New Book of Common Prayer and it was in English. An edition of this prayer book had been printed in Dublin. It was the very first book to be printed in Ireland.

The Queen of England and Ireland, Elizabeth I, was the religious leader of all her lands. She was head of the Church of England or Anglican Church. People who worshipped in this Church were known as Protestants. In Ireland, as in many other countries, most of the people considered that the Pope in Rome

was the only head of the Christian Church. They were Catholics, or Roman Catholics.

But Queen Elizabeth had decided that there should be only one Church in Ireland, the Protestant Church. She ruled that everyone must use the Protestant New Book of Common Prayer, although it was written in English and not all Irish people could understand it. She said that everyone must attend the Protestant Church of Ireland or pay a fine of one shilling each Sunday.

The Gaelic Irish and the old Anglo-Irish did not like the order to change their religion. They wanted to stay Catholic. The Pope said that they did not have to obey a king or queen who was not a Catholic. So for the first time, religious differences between Catholics and Protestants began to cause problems in Ireland.

The Munster Rebels

Gerald, fourth Earl of Desmond, and Thomas, Earl of Ormond, were bitter enemies. They argued over everything, from borders to wine taxes. Finally, they fought each other in a great battle at Affane, a place on the river Suir. For their misbehaviour, both earls were summoned before the queen in London. And Earl Gerald was made to stay in that city for the next seven years.

In the meantime, Sir James Fitzmaurice became leader of the people of Desmond. But before long, worrying rumours reached Ireland from the English court. These caused Sir James to react angrily. "The rights of the Earl of Desmond are in danger," he cried to his followers, "and I must do something about it!" The answer, he decided, was rebellion!

Sir James certainly wanted to help his uncle. But he was also a devout Catholic. So he fought not only for his uncle's rights, but also for the Catholic cause. Unfortunately the rebellion was a failure, and Sir James was forced to flee to Europe.

But on July 18th 1579, Sir James returned. He planned to stir up a second rebellion in Munster, and this time he intended to win! Help had been promised from certain noble Spanish and Italian Catholics. And the Earl of Desmond, who had at last returned from London, was on his side too. But once again, the rebellion failed

and this time Sir James and his uncle were killed.

The English could not let this happen again. They decided that the best way to stop rebellion was to remove the Irish from their land, and put English settlers in their place. So English families were settled, or 'planted' on Munster land. But this 'plantation' did not work well. However, in years to come, this way of controlling Ireland would be tried over and over again.

The pirate queen

Grace O'Malley gazed thoughtfully from one of the windows of Rochfleet castle across the calm waters of Clew Bay. She could see her fleet of galleys moored in the shelter of the hills. They had been there for nearly a month since returning from a trip to the trading ports along the coasts of Spain and Portugal. On the way back, her captains had robbed two French vessels, piling their ships with treasure. Grace had been pleased with this pirate trickery.

Now her captains and army of 200 fighting men had been sent home while Grace planned

a future raid, this time on the trading ships of the Galway merchants. But a problem had arisen. Sir Richard Bingham, the English Governor of Connacht, had gone too far! This troublesome Englishman, acting on orders from Queen Elizabeth I of England, had sent his ships to block her fleet. He had seized Grace's herds of cattle and horses, herds which had taken years to breed. He had imprisoned her son Toby for helping her, and now the man was insisting that his soldiers travel on her ships. He was trying to stop her from trading, trying to stop Grace O'Malley — chieftain of the O'Malleys, successful sea captain, and conqueror of Galway merchants and English Governors alike!

Grace pressed her lips together in determination. She would stop this once and for all. She would go to London and face this English queen. She would demand the freedom of her son, a free pardon for her past deeds, and permission to continue her pirate trade at sea. In return she would offer Elizabeth support in any sea battles against England's enemies.

Grace O'Malley, the pirate queen met Elizabeth, Queen of England, at Greenwich Palace in September 1593. Grace got her way!

O'Neill's last stand!

It was good to sit in the sun and share memories with old friends. Hugh O'Neill was a long way from home. He was an exile, living in Rome, a city in Italy.

"Never fear, we'll go back. We'll have good days in Ireland yet," Hugh O'Neill told his friends.

But he was wrong, for the great Hugh O'Neill would never see Ireland again. He would end his life in Rome.

Hugh O'Neill was born in Ulster, but as a small boy he was taken to the Pale. He was brought up in a noble household, and became a loyal subject of Queen Elizabeth.

O'Neill would have remained loyal, but Elizabeth sent English troops to Ireland to threaten his beloved Ulster. Hugh hated to see garrisons of English soldiers springing up all over his homeland. His anger was shared by another Earl, Red Hugh O'Donnell of Tyrconnell, and together they determined to beat back the English.

Then a new fort was built on the Blackwater, and 4,000 English soldiers were sent to man it. Hugh O'Neill challenged this great army at Yellow Ford, and heavily defeated it. It was the worst defeat an English army had ever experienced in Ireland! In the years to come, Hugh O'Neill and Red Hugh O'Donnell tried to win more support. They wanted to unite the Irish lords against the English. But they didn't succeed. And at last, Queen Elizabeth sent Lord Mountjoy, a stern soldier, to deal with them. Mountjoy was ruthless. He used his armies to starve out and kill O'Neill's people.

Hugh O'Neill was pardoned and made Earl of Tyrone. He stayed on in Ireland for a time, but he knew his days as head of the O'Neills were threatened. So in September 1607, he and Red Hugh O'Donnell sailed quietly away from Ireland and made their way to Italy.

It was the end of the powerful rule of the great Gaelic lords. The whole of Ireland was now under English rule.

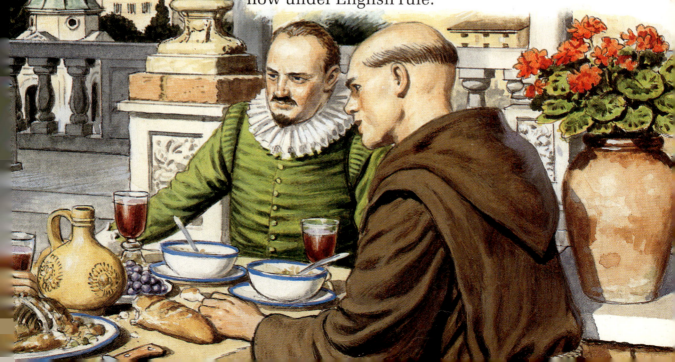

Ulster planted

In the year 1607 the two great Earls, Tyrone and Tyrconnell, left Ireland to live in exile in Italy. Their Irish lands were soon confiscated by the English government. This large area of Ireland was in Ulster. It was easy to see that Irishmen could not be turned into loyal Englishmen, so the English government decided to invite loyal Scottish and English Protestants to go there to work the land.

Some of these settlers were called undertakers, because they undertook to keep the conditions written down in their land grants. They were supposed to invite Scottish or English tenants to accompany them.

This scheme did not work very well. The undertakers usually allowed the Irish tenants to stay on because this was much cheaper than bringing over new tenants from their own countries. So Ulster did not become a Protestant province as the English king, James I, wanted. It continued to be home for a mixture of Catholics and Protestants, but now, the Protestants were mostly landlords and the Catholics mostly tenants. This caused a great deal of unhappiness. The Irish Catholics felt that they had been badly treated. And the Protestants, who were mostly English or Scottish settlers, felt, in turn, that they could not trust the Catholics.

The real quarrel between the two groups was over land. Religious differences just made things much more complicated. No one could foretell that Ulster would suffer these quarrels and problems for centuries to come.

Transported

The three stern Roundhead soldiers stood watching as the last pieces of furniture were loaded on to the wagon. These were the soldiers of the English general, Oliver Cromwell, who had been sent to Ireland in 1650. They shifted their feet impatiently as the family said tearful farewells to their ragged farmworkers. Finally, unable to wait any longer, the Roundhead officer barked an order. "Enough! You must go now. We have other houses to visit today. The new owners will soon be here."

The family climbed reluctantly on to the wagon. A whip cracked and the horses began their long, westward journey. As the wagon lumbered away, the tearful children waved goodbye to the farmworkers, but their parents did not look back.

This scene was repeated hundreds of times. After cruelly defeating the Irish, Cromwell had ordered that some of the Catholic landowners and their families who lived in the east had to leave their lands. They were forced to move west over the River Shannon, to settle in County Clare and Connacht. Their lands were then taken over by Protestants, most of whom were Cromwell's soldiers and the Adventurers — English merchants who had provided the money for the expedition to Ireland. The farmers, peasants and farmworkers who owned no land were forced to become tenants of the new owners and to work for them. The Catholics called these events the 'curse of Cromwell'.

Living off the land

Like many European peasants, the peasants in Ireland were poor and had to work hard.

For many, life under their new Protestant landlords was not always easy. But the land was fertile. And although some of the landlords preferred to stay in England and charge high rents, many others moved to their new lands and tried to improve them.

Most peasants lived in small houses or huts made from mud and stone. Most had earth floors, and the roof was usually thatched. Few homes had proper fireplaces or chimneys.

By 1750 the potato had become the main food of the Irish.

Peasants dug peat from the bogs for their fuel. It was stacked in piles to dry, then carried home by cart.

The peasants ate oatmeal, milk and a wide range of vegetables. If they lived near the sea, they caught fish and gathered shellfish. They used boats called curraghs made from hides painted with tar and stretched over a wooden frame. These looked flimsy but were very strong and seaworthy. Where the land was poor, seaweed was used as a fertilizer.

The landlords preferred to raise cattle rather than grow crops. The peasants usually tended the cattle.

Dublin docks

The captain watched the last of the barrels being swung into the hold of his ship. "Just right for the tide," he thought, with a grunt of satisfaction, "and the wind is set fair for Liverpool. It will be a quick and easy passage."

Walking to the rail, he looked down on the crowded dock. Carts clattered along, laden with bales of wool, timber for barrel-making, hides, sides of beef and boxes of fish. A voice broke into his day-dream. "The cargo is secure, sir." He turned to the saluting officer. "Very well, Mr Mulligan. Set the sails and stand by to cast off."

At that time, many Irishmen from different backgrounds were merchants and traders. For the Gaelic Irish, it was the only way to become powerful, as they were not allowed to enter politics. The merchants helped ports like

Dublin, Cork, Waterford, Galway, Limerick and Kinsale to grow. Into these harbours came sugar from the West Indies and flax from America, as well as goods from England — fine cloth and hops for making beer.

Much of the wealth of these ports came from selling supplies such as beef, butter, whiskey, horses and barrels to the English Navy. By 1697, the streets of Dublin were lit at night, a sign of a wealthy city.

Trade became so great that in the 1780s a grand Customs House was built on Dublin dock. Here, goods were unloaded from ships that tied up at the quay. Customs officers collected a tax called duty on every item that came ashore. Trade grew and grew. The city merchants became very wealthy and there were many new jobs for other people.

King James comes to Ireland

The crowds cheered loudly. Bells rang, pipes played, guns were fired into the air. The mayor and other leaders of Dublin stepped forward to greet King James as he entered the city. At last, they thought, there was a Catholic ruler in Ireland. Surely he would help the Irish Catholics!

The English Parliament had refused to allow James II to continue ruling as king because he was a Catholic. Instead, they offered the throne of England to William, Prince of Orange, who was a Dutch Protestant. William gladly accepted the offer. When he arrived in England from the Netherlands to take the crown, James decided to flee. He crossed quickly to Ireland where he knew he would be welcomed by the Catholic population.

In 1689, he formed a Parliament and declared himself king of Ireland. But James couldn't do very much to help the people. The Catholics wanted him to return the lands which Cromwell had taken away from them. They wanted him to make the Catholic Church the official Church of Ireland again. But James always remembered that he was also the rightful king of England. He could not agree to do anything that might harm England, even though the Irish Catholics offered to fight for him. Also he was very short of money. Within a year of his arrival, James was preparing to flee from his new kingdom, for William's army had landed in Ireland to win back control.

The Battle of the Boyne

The young soldier stood stiffly to attention, his musket by his side. He could feel beads of sweat running down his forehead. His hands felt clammy. Ahead of him, he saw the Catholic troops, gathered on the banks of the river Boyne. There seemed so many of them! He looked around him, and soon picked out

the figure of the man who was his leader. King William of Orange looked proud and confident. Suddenly the soldier heard the roar of cannons and the whistle of the cannon balls as they flew towards him. He stood his ground. The air became dark with smoke and men began to shout.

"This is it!" the soldier thought. "The battle has really begun."

Little did the soldier know how important this battle was to be. The troops of William of Orange, who were mainly Protestant, joined battle with the troops of James II, who were mostly Catholic.

The Battle of the Boyne raged throughout the day of July 1st 1690. The Protestant army finally won, and King James was forced to turn and run. He left Ireland as quickly as he could and sailed to France.

This was a historic victory. The Protestants were soon to be firmly in charge of the country.

The night attack

"Charge!"

Out of the darkness thundered five hundred grim-faced riders, led by Patrick Sarsfield, earl of Lucan. Their sabres flashed in the light of the camp-fires as they galloped past the tents of the astonished English, Dutch and Irish soldiers. Soon they reached the carts and guns of the siege train they had come to destroy.

In a few moments, the battle was over. The carts loaded with gunpowder were blazing. Sarsfield's riders raced into the night, leaving chaos behind them. A few seconds later, there was a flash and an enormous explosion which awoke people sleeping in distant villages. The huge siege guns, which should have been used to attack Limerick, were blown sky-high. For the moment, the city was safe.

But Sarsfield's brave attack on the siege train was not enough to save the Catholic Irish. King William's army won several other battles and finally captured Limerick a year later, in October 1691.

Soldiers from Catholic France arrived too late to help the Catholic Irish. Sarsfield had just signed a peace treaty called the Treaty of Limerick. The Irish might have continued to fight but Sarsfield was an honourable man. He had agreed to surrender and so, just as he had promised, the Irish soldiers who had supported King James II laid down their arms.

King William wanted these brave soldiers to join his army, but most decided to go back with the French, and so they left the country they loved. Many of them never returned.

The Wild Geese

It was the night before the battle, and the French army was asleep. No one seemed to be awake except for a small group of young Irish soldiers huddled round a flickering camp-fire. One of them began to sing softly of the green hills of Ireland, and quietly, the others joined in the chorus.

They were remembering their homeland. Many knew that they would never see Ireland or their families again. If they were not killed in this battle, they would be killed in another, and so would be buried in foreign soil.

These Irish soldiers were the Wild Geese, members of Sarsfield's army. They had left Ireland to live in foreign lands, as they had agreed to do in the Treaty of Limerick. Many other Irishmen became 'soldiers of fortune' too. These soldiers travelled all over the world, joining foreign armies to fight alongside the enemies of England. This was their way of taking revenge for the treatment Ireland had suffered at the hands of the English. Many were killed. Nearly half a million Irish soldiers died fighting in France alone.

But although the Wild Geese fought under foreign banners in faraway places, they never forgot they were Irish.

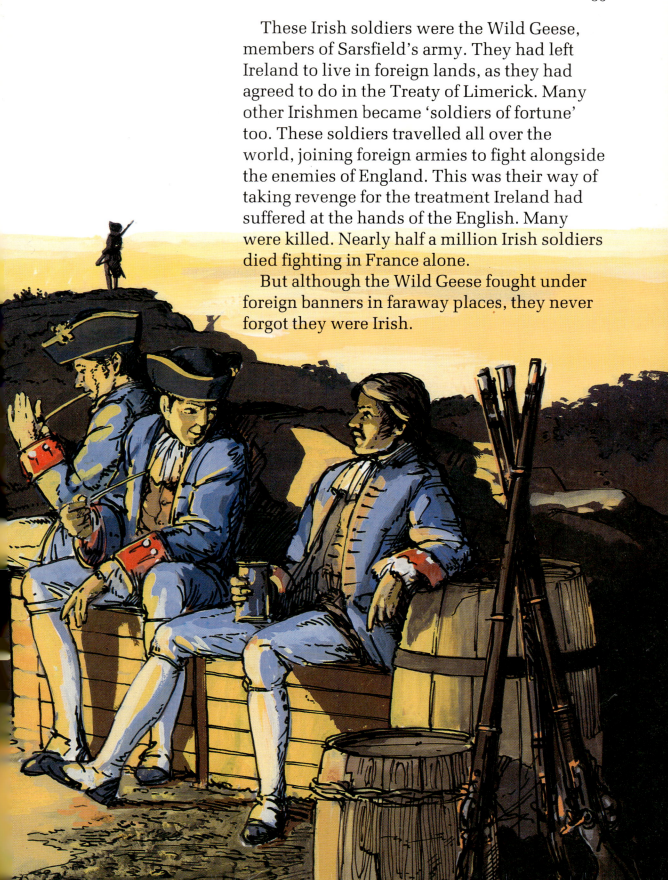

The penal laws

The young priest hung on grimly as the cart lurched violently. He wiped the rain from his face and glanced at the bishop beside him, shivering in his rain-soaked cloak. "The old man looks ill," the priest thought. "Will we reach the ship in time?" But he knew they could go no faster. They had already slid into a ditch, which had delayed them for an hour.

The bishop was fleeing from Ireland because of some new laws, called the penal laws. These strict rules against the Catholic Church had been introduced by the English and Irish Parliaments after William III was made king.

The penal laws said that all bishops, archbishops, Catholics of the Jesuit order, friars and monks had to leave Ireland by May 1st 1698. The punishment for returning was death. The Protestant Parliament hoped that the Catholic Church would die out because of these laws.

But it didn't. In fact, the penal laws made the Catholic Church stronger, because it was difficult to make sure that the laws were carried out. Many Protestants actually helped Catholics to get round the laws. The punishment of death was never used. Parish priests were left alone, although they had to be registered and promise good behaviour. As well as this, some unregistered priests stayed in Ireland, living in hiding and holding secret masses. This kept the Catholic faith alive.

The fiddle and the pipe

"Here he is," cried the young girl with glee. "It's the dancing master."

She opened the door of the cottage to welcome her teacher. With him came a piper and a fiddler to play the violin. The piper might play a Uilleann pipe, pumping air into a bag to sound the notes. He might play the flute or even the penny whistle.

As quickly as possible, a space was cleared and the lesson began. The girl concentrated on learning the steps of the 'Balrudery', the 'Whip of Dunboyne', and the 'Irish Trot'. She was determined to be the best dancer at the regular Sunday dance!

In the 1700s and 1800s, dancing was very popular, especially among the poorer people.

Dancing masters travelled throughout the country. They went from one cottage to another, charging a few pence for a quarter hour's lesson.

Almost every Sunday, there would be a dance in one of the villages or small towns. The country people would walk great distances to get there. The piper and fiddler would play, and the men and women would dance jigs, reels and country dances like the 'Morning Brush'. Sometimes couples would dance the 'Cake Dance'. The cake in the centre of the skipping circle would be awarded to the couple who stayed on their feet the longest.

There was plenty of dancing in the wealthier homes too. Dances took place in large drawing rooms, or ballrooms. The dances were called 'soirées dansantes' and many people attended. Formation dances like the minuet and the cotillion were very popular. Dancing in the evening was thought to put right everything that had gone wrong during the day!

Jonathan Swift

"Here comes the Dean!"

The cry went up and was passed down the street. Beggars and other poor folk swarmed round a black-clad figure striding towards St Patrick's cathedral.

The Dean kept taking money from his pockets and pressing coins into the outstretched hands. He hardly paused to hear the grateful thanks which followed him as he passed.

This was Jonathan Swift, Dean of the Cathedral of St Patrick, giving charity to the poor of Dublin. He was well-known and respected throughout the city. He lived very simply, saving his money to give to the poor. He set up a charity home, or almshouse, where needy widows could find shelter. He also

founded a school for poor children.

Swift was even better known as a writer. His most famous book was 'Gulliver's Travels', the story of a man who meets many adventures in lands where strange giants and little people roam. He also wrote many letters and articles which criticized the way in which the English Parliament treated Ireland.

Although many of his articles contained bitter attacks, they were often very amusing as well. He became a very popular writer and people eagerly awaited his latest writing.

Although he was born in Dublin, Swift had English parents. More than anything, he wanted to live in England, and he always claimed to hate Ireland. However, he hated unfairness even more, and so this bad-tempered but much-loved man became a champion of the Irish people. It was said that when he died in 1745, a hush fell over the whole city of Dublin.

The blind harper

The blind harper bowed amidst thunderous applause. The crowd cheered and called on him to sing another song. As soon as he struck his harp, a hush fell. His silent audience listened closely to the Gaelic words.

As he sang of a beautiful maiden called Erin, they all knew he was really singing about Ireland. And when he sang of her lover who had fled to escape a cruel lord, they all knew he was singing about the sons of Ireland who had gone abroad to find a better life. His whole song was the history of Ireland.

The poet was Turlough O'Carolan, who had been blind since the age of twenty-two. He was one of Ireland's wandering poets. Most poets wrote down their poetry, but a few, like Turlough, sang it as well. These poets often met together to listen to each other's works. Some were entertained in the homes of the rich. Others travelled around, reciting and singing in the villages.

The poets always wrote in Gaelic, the original Irish language, and they tried to keep the traditions of the Irish people alive. Their most enthusiastic audiences were in the west, among the Catholic families who had been transported there by Cromwell.

The poets wrote about love, about nature, and about their rich patrons. As well as songs of politics and patriotism, they wrote tales that made fun of their enemies. Many of these became very popular and were passed down by word of mouth. Some of them can still be heard today.

The Whiteboys

There was a rasp of flint against steel and a torch burst into flame. "Forward!" came the cry, and the trees seemed to come alive with shadowy white-shirted figures, wearing white scarves over their faces. They raced across the field, vaulted over the wall and ran towards the farmhouse.

One group smashed down the fence with axes and drove the cattle away. Another group began setting light to the barns and hayricks. As the flames roared upwards, the farmer and his family fled panic-stricken through the back door of the farmhouse and ran across the fields to safety. Seeing them go, the attackers threw their torches into the house and cheered as the flames took hold.

The attackers were called the Whiteboys. They were just one of several secret societies which sprang up in Ireland during the eighteenth century. Many were Catholic, but others, like the Oakboys and the Steelboys, were Presbyterian.

These secret societies were formed to protect poor farmworkers from their landlords. The societies protested about high rents and attacked landlords who treated their workers unfairly. They burned buildings, drove off the cattle and even committed murder.

All the Members of the Irish Parliament were Protestant so the Catholic peasants had no one to stand up for them. They looked to the secret societies for help. Those who joined a society had to swear a secret oath and obey the rules. There were harsh punishments for those who broke the rules.

Dublin and its Parliament

Sir Edward Pearce, the architect, arrived at the building site very early in the morning. He wanted to check the builders' progress, so he carried the plans of the new Parliament building under his arm.

He walked through the arches until he stood under the magnificent dome of the House of Commons. His footsteps echoed as he paced across the octagonal chamber. "Soon," he thought,

"Ireland will have a Parliament building that will be the envy of Europe."

Edward Pearce's Parliament building was finished in 1739. It was just one of hundreds of fine buildings which were built in Dublin and the rest of Ireland in the early eighteenth century.

Dublin had been overcrowded and dirty, but trade had brought wealth to the city. The rich merchants began to build fine houses for themselves. Streets were widened and elegant squares were laid out. Those who could afford carriages were able to drive through the tree-lined avenues of Phoenix Park.

Outside the city, the wealthy landowners copied the European style of architecture, and built magnificent country houses set in parks with lakes and gardens. The houses were filled with the finest furniture, pictures, china and silverware that money could buy.

The rich enjoyed their new life. They went to balls, parties, plays and concerts. Dublin became second only to London as a centre for fashion and elegance.

The Irish Volunteers

The windows of the houses around College Green were filled with people waving and cheering as the Volunteers marched into the square.

"Present muskets!" shouted an officer. "Fire!" The shots rang out and a cloud of smoke rolled over the scene.

This parade of the Volunteers took place in Dublin in 1779. The Volunteers were formed when British troops left Ireland to fight in the American War of Independence. Without troops to protect them from a possible French

invasion, the Irish Protestants decided to form bands of volunteer soldiers.

The Americans had begun their revolution in 1775. They complained that they had to pay heavy taxes to Britain, but had no say in their own government.

Many of the Irish supported the American idea of rebelling against Britain. They, too, complained about the taxes they had to pay. Their complaints grew louder when the British passed laws to stop Irish trade with America.

Before long the Volunteers were demanding that the British should allow Irish merchants to trade freely. Later, they began to demand that Ireland should be altogether free from British rule.

1. Sheep grazed in many parts of Ireland.

2. The wool was clipped by sheep shearers.

Irish wool

The British Prime Minister, Lord North, was worried. It was 1779. The Americans were rebelling, and the French were threatening to attack Britain. The Irish Volunteers were beginning to look dangerous as well.

Lord North decided that something had to be done to calm the Irish. So in 1780, he announced that Irish merchants would be allowed to trade freely with other countries.

One of the industries which did well from free trade was wool. This was a small but important industry in Ireland. Much of the work could be done by the peasants in their own homes. In this way, poor families could earn a little extra money for food.

3. The fleeces were washed with fuller's earth, a powder which took out the grease and dirt.

6. The wool was dyed.

5. The wool was spun on spinning wheels. The strands of wool twisted on the spindle into a strong thread.

4. The wool was carded, or combed with spiked pads, to get rid of the tangles.

7. The woollen thread was woven into cloth on a loom.

8. Most of the cloth was sold in Ireland. Some was packed into bales, loaded on to ships and sold abroad.

Grattan's Parliament

"I am now to address a free people. Ireland is now a nation!" The speaker sat down. Cheers echoed round the domed roof of the Irish House of Commons. The Members of Parliament rose to their feet, waving and shouting.

It was 1782 and a new feeling of confidence was sweeping through the Protestants of Ireland. For a long time it had not been easy for the Irish Parliament to pass laws, because the British Parliament held this power. The Irish

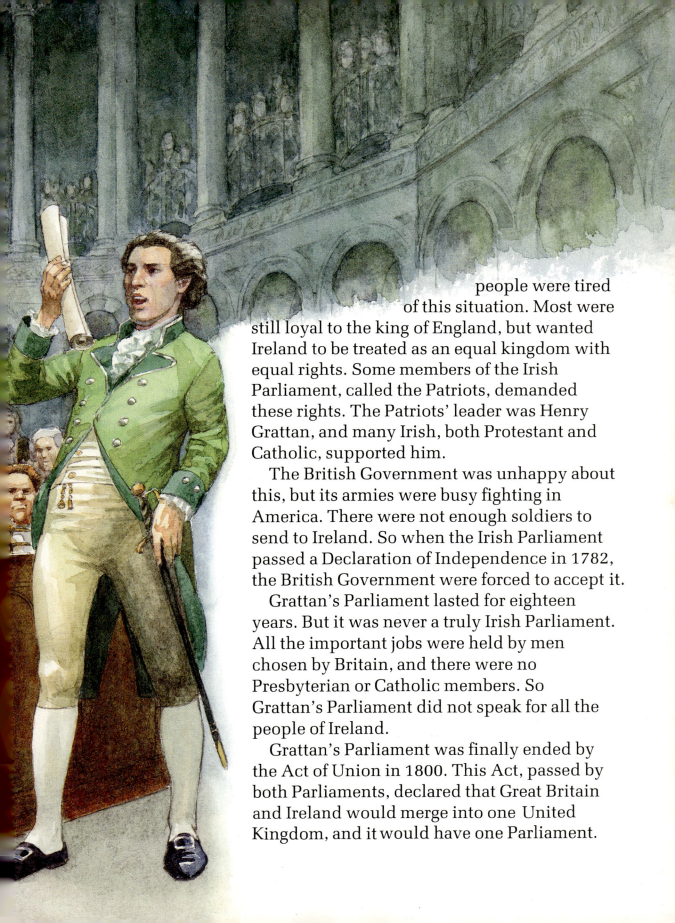

people were tired of this situation. Most were still loyal to the king of England, but wanted Ireland to be treated as an equal kingdom with equal rights. Some members of the Irish Parliament, called the Patriots, demanded these rights. The Patriots' leader was Henry Grattan, and many Irish, both Protestant and Catholic, supported him.

The British Government was unhappy about this, but its armies were busy fighting in America. There were not enough soldiers to send to Ireland. So when the Irish Parliament passed a Declaration of Independence in 1782, the British Government were forced to accept it.

Grattan's Parliament lasted for eighteen years. But it was never a truly Irish Parliament. All the important jobs were held by men chosen by Britain, and there were no Presbyterian or Catholic members. So Grattan's Parliament did not speak for all the people of Ireland.

Grattan's Parliament was finally ended by the Act of Union in 1800. This Act, passed by both Parliaments, declared that Great Britain and Ireland would merge into one United Kingdom, and it would have one Parliament.

Bantry Bay

The gale lashed the coast of south-west Ireland. It whipped the surface of the water in Bantry Bay. The rain drove down on the ships as they heaved and tossed. The wind shrieked through the rigging as the French sailors struggled desperately with the sails. At last the Captain turned to the young Irishman beside him. He shouted above the roar of the storm.

"It's no good, Monsieur. We must give up now or we will all sink." Sadly, Wolfe Tone nodded in agreement. The signal was given to turn back and the ships, packed with French soldiers, began their voyage back to France.

It was Christmas Day, in the year 1796. Wolfe Tone, a young Dublin Protestant, was a member of the United Irishmen. This secret society wanted to bring together all the Irish people. They wanted Protestants and Catholics to join together in forming one nation. They plotted a rebellion against the Government in Ireland. Wolfe Tone went to France to ask the French to send soldiers to help him and his fellow rebels. Had it not been for the storm in Bantry Bay, the plot of the United Irishmen might have succeeded.

Although the Irish Government had had a lucky escape, it was very frightened by this plot. It decided to put an end to the United Irishmen once and for all. It sent an army to scour the countryside and round up the rebels.

The government soldiers behaved very cruelly as they tried to get information from the peasants. In the end, the terrified people came to hate the government and its soldiers. Another rebellion was in the making!

The United Irishmen

Lord Edward's eyes opened suddenly. Was that a noise he had heard outside? He sat up on the bed where he had been resting. Suddenly there was a loud crash. The door burst open and some men rushed in. It was the police!

Lord Edward sprang off the bed and drew his knife. As the police threw themselves upon him, he stabbed wildly, killing one of the officers. Then a shot rang out and he slumped, bleeding, to the floor.

Lord Edward Fitzgerald, an Irish nobleman, had been an officer in the British army. But by 1798, he was sympathetic to the cause of the United Irishmen and had become a member of a secret group called the Directory. This band of men led the United Irishmen in a plot to overthrow the Irish Government.

The Irish Government had not forgotten the plot of 1796 when Wolfe Tone had nearly reached Ireland with an army of French soldiers. When its spies reported that a second rebellion was planned, it decided to arrest all the members of the Directory at once.

The police quickly captured Lord Edward's friends but he himself managed to escape. He had hidden in the house of a Dublin leather merchant, and it was here that the police eventually found him. Lord Edward's gunshot wound was very bad. He was imprisoned for being one of the leaders of the United Irishmen but before he could be brought to trial, he died.

Vinegar Hill

The sun blazed down on Vinegar Hill. The green rebel flag flew from an old windmill on one side of the hill. The sun glinted on the bayonets of the troops as they lined up at the bottom of the slope.

Then the cannons began to fire. Shells exploded. Muskets cracked, and smoke rolled across the scene. With a great shout, the government troops charged up the slope. The rebels retreated, but more army troops were waiting for them. A terrible massacre followed. Only a few rebels managed to escape, and the rebellion in Wexford was over.

Before the day of the battle in 1798, Vinegar Hill in Wexford had been the main rebel camp.

Many peasants had gathered there. Some came to fight, but most wanted to escape the cruelty of the army who were searching for rebels in the neighbouring countryside. They played music and sang songs to keep up their spirits. They sat around on furniture and carpets which they had stolen from nearby towns. They had even stolen cattle to feed the people in the camp.

After the defeat at Vinegar Hill, the rebels were never as strong again. Soon after, the Protestants attempted a further uprising in Ulster, but it too, ended in failure. And in August, a French force actually landed in Ireland. It won its first battle, but without rebel help it gave in and surrendered. Wolfe Tone arrived with more French ships. But he was captured and died soon after. This ended the hopes of the United Irishmen for ever.

Daniel O'Connell

Daniel O'Connell rose to his feet. He stood on a platform on the top of the hill, looking down at a huge crowd. There were over three quarters of a million people all watching him expectantly. It was his biggest meeting yet!

This great gathering took place on the Royal Hill of Tara in August 1843. Daniel O'Connell was a Catholic lawyer and gentleman. Fourteen years earlier, he had become well-known and very popular. He had organized a campaign against a law which said that no Catholic could be a Member of Parliament. In 1829, O'Connell challenged this law by standing as a candidate for County Clare. He won with a large majority of votes. Rather than risk a rebellion in Ireland, the British Government agreed to change the law. This meant that any Roman Catholic could be a Member of Parliament. This was called Catholic Emancipation.

O'Connell hated fighting and violence, and he was glad that the government had given in to a peaceful protest. His followers called him the Liberator. In 1843 he took up another challenge. He organized what were called 'monster rallies' to persuade the British Government that the Irish people wanted their own separate Parliament again. But this time the government was not frightened, and dared him to provoke a civil war. But O'Connell remained true to his love of peaceful methods, and told his followers to return quietly to their homes. Even so, he went to prison for a while.

Daniel O'Connell died in 1847. His work was not finished, but he had shown how strong Irish Catholics could be when they worked together. However, very few Protestants supported him. When he visited Belfast, where many Protestants lived, he had to flee from his hotel in disguise. Despite his good intentions, he could not unite all the Irish people.

The potato famine

Liam had been working in the field since dawn, digging deeply into the raised furrows where the potato plants had grown. There was just a chance that some of the potatoes had escaped the disease, and Liam had hoped and prayed that this might be so. But almost all the potatoes he'd found had been black and pulpy, and had squelched to nothing in his hand. He'd put the best potatoes in his basket, but even these smelled rotten.

By the middle of the nineteenth century, the population of Ireland had risen to about eight million. And about half of those people lived almost entirely on potatoes. If anything were to go wrong with the potato crop it would be a disaster! In fact, in 1816, the crop had partially failed and there had been famine in some areas. But so far, the population had survived.

Then, in 1845, the unthinkable happened!

In August of that year, the crops had looked good. But by September, black spots were seen developing on the leaves of the plants. Soon, a white mould coated the underside of each leaf. A killer fungus, or blight, was attacking the crops. The blight quickly spread from one plant to another, and soon it became obvious that the country's entire potato crop was diseased.

At first, the main fear was starvation. However, another problem soon arose. When people were weak from hunger, they could not fight disease. Many died of sickness and fever.

Thousands of people decided to leave their homes in Ireland and emigrate to new lands. They packed into emigration ships that were so overcrowded that many passengers died.

Leaving for America

A small boat was sailing towards the ship, picking its way through the busy waters of New York harbour.

The ship was filled with immigrants, people who had left their homes in other countries to come and live in America. The immigrants lining the rails watched the boat approach. " 'Tis the immigration officers," they muttered. "It won't be long now before we're Americans."

Immigration from Ireland to the United States began in the eighteenth century. The first ships reached Boston in 1718. But during the nineteenth century, immigrants arrived in America from many parts of the world. When they landed, they were divided into groups. Then they shuffled in long queues past doctors and nurses.

They were questioned. Where had they come from? How many children did they have? Could they read and write? They were examined by the medical staff. Some had letters chalked on their backs. 'H' stood for heart disease, 'E' for eye trouble, and 'F' for a face rash.

Some were refused entry for medical reasons. Those who were accepted went through a door labelled 'Push for New York'. On the other side they found themselves in the hustle and bustle of their new city home.

Most Irish immigrants were very poor. They mostly found jobs in cloth factories, working long hours for little pay. They lived in overcrowded apartments paying high rents. Still, they were rich compared to their relations in Ireland. They kept in touch by letter and sent money home.

Today, many millions of Americans can trace their families back to these immigrant ships. Most people are leading successful, happy lives, but they never forget their roots in Ireland.

Eviction

"Open up! Open up!"

The children ran to hide behind their mother's skirt, frightened by the loud knocking on the door. The sheriff sat outside on his horse, surrounded by a group of policemen and a gang of roughly-dressed workmen carrying iron bars.

"Please don't touch our home," sobbed the mother. The sheriff took no notice. He gave a signal and the men went into the house. After throwing the family's few possessions into the road, they began to tear off the roof. Within a few minutes only the bare walls were left.

It was 1848 and the potato harvest had failed again. The Irish people asked the British Government for help. But the British had already spent millions of pounds helping

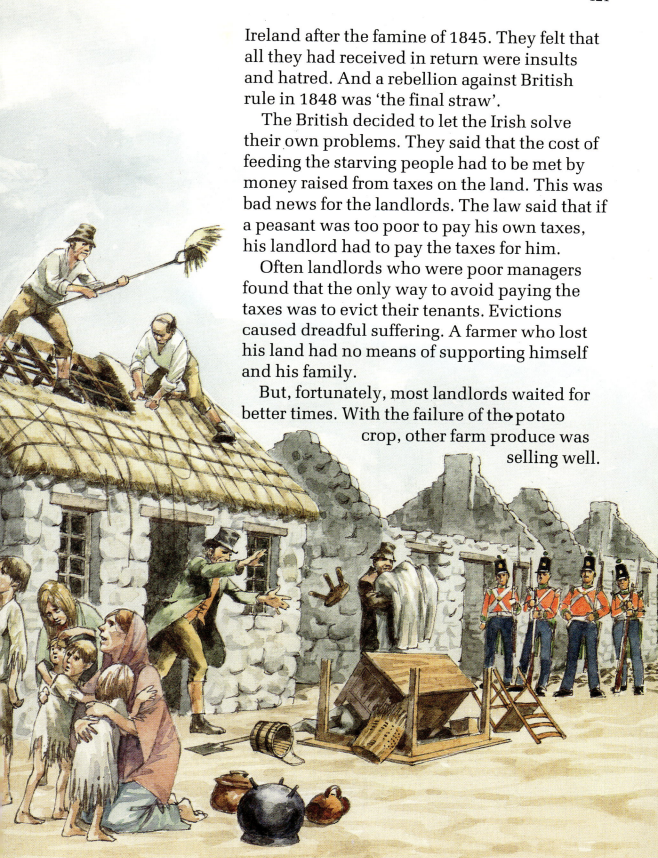

Ireland after the famine of 1845. They felt that all they had received in return were insults and hatred. And a rebellion against British rule in 1848 was 'the final straw'.

The British decided to let the Irish solve their own problems. They said that the cost of feeding the starving people had to be met by money raised from taxes on the land. This was bad news for the landlords. The law said that if a peasant was too poor to pay his own taxes, his landlord had to pay the taxes for him.

Often landlords who were poor managers found that the only way to avoid paying the taxes was to evict their tenants. Evictions caused dreadful suffering. A farmer who lost his land had no means of supporting himself and his family.

But, fortunately, most landlords waited for better times. With the failure of the potato crop, other farm produce was selling well.

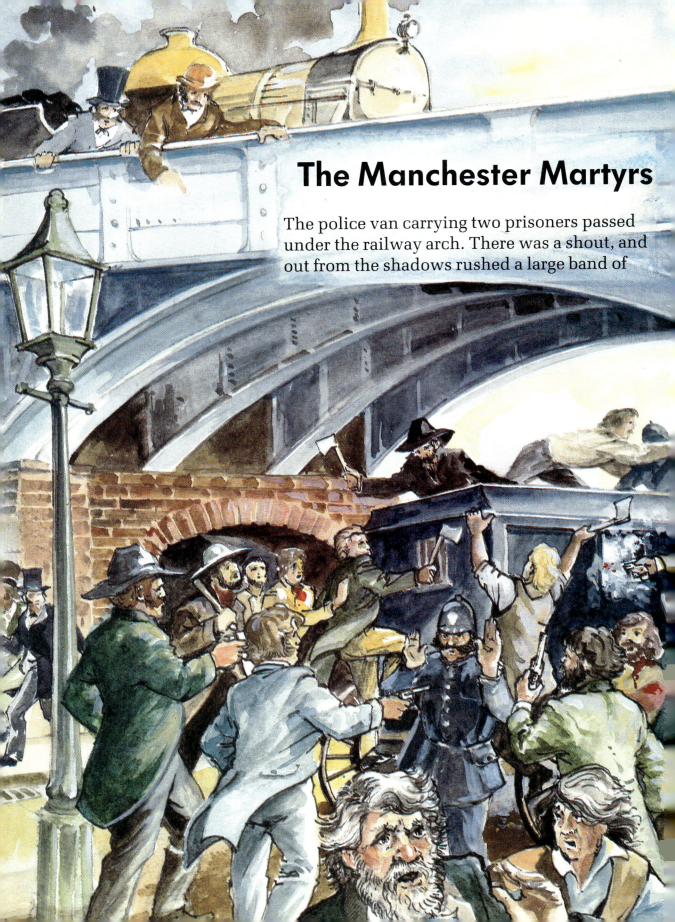

The Manchester Martyrs

The police van carrying two prisoners passed under the railway arch. There was a shout, and out from the shadows rushed a large band of

men. Brandishing revolvers, they forced the unarmed police to climb down from the van. Then they set about opening the doors to release the prisoners.

"Surrender!" they shouted through the ventilator, pointing their pistols at Sergeant Brett inside the van. "Never!" came his reply. Then a shot rang out and the sergeant fell dying to the floor. The key was passed out and soon the two prisoners, Kelly and Deasy, had escaped from the van and were crossing the railway.

These events took place in Manchester in 1866. Kelly and Deasy were not recaptured, but five other Irishmen were arrested and brought to trial. They were accused of murdering Sergeant Brett, and of being Fenians.

The Fenians were members of a secret society formed during the 1860s. The society planned to overthrow British rule in Ireland. It had carried out a series of bomb attacks in Britain. The British Government was now determined to put a stop to its activities.

Three of the accused men, Allen, Larkin and O'Brien, had indeed taken part in the attack. Although none of them had actually fired the shot that killed the sergeant, all three were sentenced to be hanged. They were executed in public one foggy morning in November 1867. Many Irish people felt that Sergeant Brett's death had been an accident and that hanging was too harsh a penalty. The three became known as the 'Manchester Martyrs'. Their deaths caused many Irish people to give their support to the Fenians.

Factory workers

It was a dark, cold morning in Belfast. Groups of workers began to leave their houses and shuffle through the cobbled streets. The women pulled their shawls tightly round their shoulders. Many of the men were coughing.

The air seemed thick and heavy. The stink of factory smoke and open sewers hung over the city. A distant train puffed along slowly. The Industrial Revolution had come to Ireland. In the eighteenth century, most people in Ireland lived and worked on the land. But between about 1780 to 1850, the lives of many people changed. During this period, all kinds of machines were invented to make new products, mostly in huge factories. The goods were transported by new roads and railways. Docks expanded as more and more goods were traded overseas. Hundreds of thousands of people left the country to work in the fast-growing cities and towns.

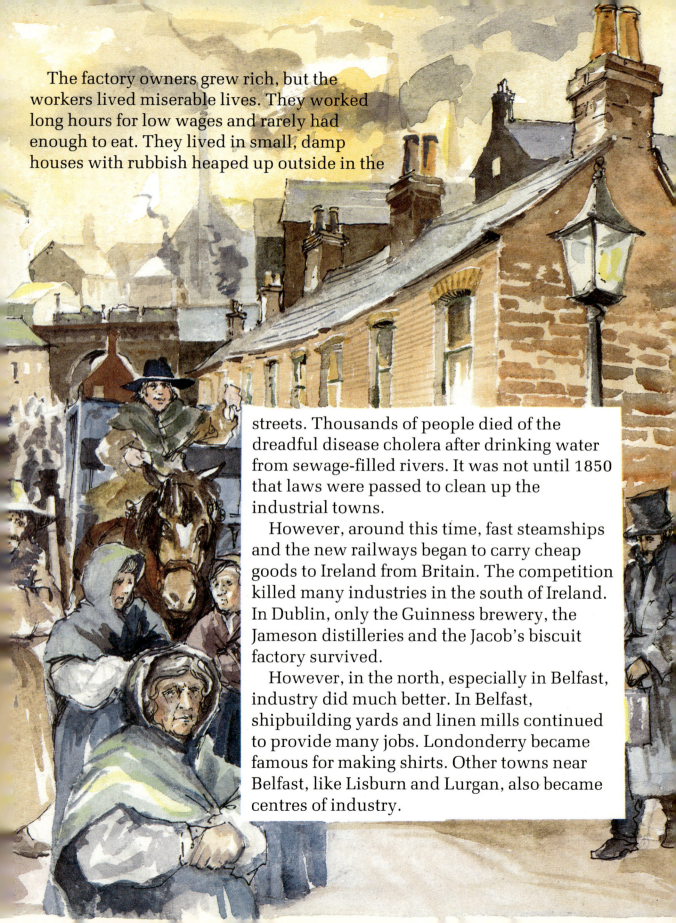

The factory owners grew rich, but the workers lived miserable lives. They worked long hours for low wages and rarely had enough to eat. They lived in small, damp houses with rubbish heaped up outside in the streets. Thousands of people died of the dreadful disease cholera after drinking water from sewage-filled rivers. It was not until 1850 that laws were passed to clean up the industrial towns.

However, around this time, fast steamships and the new railways began to carry cheap goods to Ireland from Britain. The competition killed many industries in the south of Ireland. In Dublin, only the Guinness brewery, the Jameson distilleries and the Jacob's biscuit factory survived.

However, in the north, especially in Belfast, industry did much better. In Belfast, shipbuilding yards and linen mills continued to provide many jobs. Londonderry became famous for making shirts. Other towns near Belfast, like Lisburn and Lurgan, also became centres of industry.

Boycott!

Neither of the two men actually owned the plot of land. The owner lived in England and never visited his estates. He rented his land to several landlords, and they in turn rented it out to tenants, usually poor farmers. The land was often looked after by a land agent.

The landlords were only interested in making money, so they put up the rents. Of course, a tenant often couldn't pay, and if that happened, he was thrown off the land. He was paid nothing for any improvements he made.

In 1879, Irish peasants banded together into a Land League to fight unfair landlords. The first president of the league was an Irish Member of the British Parliament, Charles Stewart Parnell. He suggested that instead of fighting the landlords, the peasants should ignore their demands.

In 1880, Captain Boycott, a landlord with estates in County Mayo, became the first landlord to be treated in this way. When he raised his rents, his labourers left the fields

The land agent sometimes cheated both the tenant and his employer.

just before the harvest. His servants packed their bags and departed. The postman refused to deliver his letters. The baker refused to sell him bread.

He asked the British Government for help. Fifty Protestant workers volunteered to gather his harvest and the British Government sent 2,000 soldiers to guard them.

Organized by a local priest, Father O'Malley, the people of County Mayo shut their shops and ignored the troops. Hungry and tired, the soldiers arrived at Captain Boycott's estate only to find that they had left all their tent pegs behind. Then it began to pour with rain!

This method of ignoring a landlord came to be known as a boycott.

Parnell

Charles and Fanny were playing in the
nursery. In front of each of them was a row of
toy soldiers. The children were bowling
wooden balls across the room, trying to knock
down each other's army.

After a few minutes, Fanny's army lay in
ruins. "Hurrah!" cheered Charles. "I've won!"
Fanny crossed the room, looking suspiciously
at Charles's soldiers which were all still
standing. "Why," she cried, "you've glued
them to the floor!"

Even as a child, Charles Stewart Parnell
liked to win. He was born and raised in
Ireland, the son of rich Protestant parents. At
the age of thirteen, he inherited 5,000 acres in
County Wicklow. Later he went to Cambridge
University.

In spite of being a Protestant landowner, he
took the side of the Irish peasants. Entering

British Parliament in 1875, he soon became leader of the Irish Home Rule Party — a group demanding a separate Irish Parliament.

Parnell was a powerful speaker, and it was mainly thanks to him that a Land Act to protect the Irish peasants was passed. His power and popularity grew so great that many British people began to fear him. They thought he might even be a Fenian, although he didn't openly support violence.

In 1890 he was ruined by a scandal and lost much support and popularity. Exhausted by constant travelling between London and Ireland, he became ill. At the early age of 45, he died in the arms of his wife. Some people said that all hopes of Irish Home Rule were buried with him.

The doctor who cared

The young student doctor smiled. He looked down at the beaming, scrubbed faces of the children. Just a few days ago they had been roaming the streets of London, ragged and homeless. Now they were being taken care of in the East End Mission for Destitute Children — a hostel that the young man had founded himself. The young student's name was Thomas John Barnardo.

Thomas Barnardo was born in Dublin in 1845. As he grew up he saw the squalor and poverty that existed in the slums of his city. It sickened him to see people living this way. So he decided to do what he could to help.

In 1866 he went to London. There he studied to become a medical missionary.

He was very eager to start his work among the poor, so he founded the hostel while he was still a student.

He opened his first children's home in 1870 at Stepney in London. It was to be the first of many. The homes were called Doctor Barnardo's Homes for Needy Children. The children in them were taught a trade, so that they could earn their living. They were often helped to emigrate to America, Australia and especially Canada. In these countries, they would have a better chance of making a good life for themselves.

Today, children in Ireland are helped by several other organizations too, such as the Irish Society for the Prevention of Cruelty to Children. There is also 'Care', a group that tries to make people understand the problems of Irish children in need. But all over the world, children who need help are cared for in memory of the Irish doctor, Doctor Barnardo. Today, his homes support more than 9,000 children.

Her Royal Highness, The Princess of Wales, is President of Dr Barnardo's. Here she celebrates a birthday with one of the children at the Sharonmore Project in Belfast.

Modern writers

A picture formed in the poet's mind as he started to write. He could see the lake very clearly in his imagination. On the far shore

Poems W.B. Yeats

FAIRY TALES Sinead de Valera

Flight of the Dov WALTER MACKEN

there was a small cabin where he would live. It would be made very simply from wattle and clay, and on the small plot of land around it, he would grow a few vegetables for his needs. Life would be so peaceful. There would be time to enjoy the passing of each day, time to listen to the bird's song, and cricket's chirrup. It would all be very different to life in the city.

William Butler Yeats may well have been thinking this way as he wrote 'Lake Isle of Innisfree'. It is one of many beautiful poems written by Ireland's most famous poet in praise of the Irish shores and countryside.

Yeats also wrote plays. He opened the Abbey Theatre in Dublin as a place where Irish plays could be performed. Like many other Irish writers of the time, he wanted to write about Ireland. He won the famous Nobel prize for his work.

The last hundred years have produced many great Irish writers. Perhaps the most famous are the playwright George Bernard Shaw and the novelist James Joyce. Less well-known but still very important are several short story writers such as Frank O'Connor, Sean O'Faolain, Mary Lavin and Liam O'Flaherty. Famous playwrights include John Millington Synge and Sean O'Casey.

Oscar Wilde was born on October 16th 1854 in Dublin. He is best known for his wit and for the plays that he wrote. But he was also a writer of wonderful children's stories such as 'The Happy Prince'.

This great tradition of Irish literature continues to the present day, thanks to the work of modern Irish authors, many of whom write especially for children. Edna O'Brien, Walter Machen, Bernard MacLaverty and Patricia Lynch are just a few writers of tales and poems that children will enjoy.

Island of Strangers
CATHERINE SEFTON

PORTRAIT of the ARTIST as a Young Man
JAMES JOYCE

THE HAPPY PRINCE
Oscar Wilde

Short Stories
Liam O'Flaherty

Clydevalley cargo

A powerful light cut through the darkness, throwing long shadows over the dock. The crane creaked into action, lifting the first box from the hold. Just for a moment, everyone stopped and looked. It was almost as if they were frozen by the flashlight of a camera.

Then the scene sprang to life. Groups of men hurried about the quay, lifting the long boxes into the waiting lorries. The guns had arrived.

It was the night of April 24th 1914. The ship being unloaded in Larne harbour was the S.S. Clydevalley. She was carrying a dangerous cargo of 24,000 rifles and over three million bullets. They had come to Ireland from Germany. The rifles had been bought by the Ulster Unionists.

For several years the British Government had been considering Home Rule for Ireland — allowing Ireland to rule itself. The Ulster Unionists wanted Ireland to remain part of Britain. Their leader, Sir Edward Carson, a Dubliner, had warned that they were ready to fight to get their way. In 1912, the Unionists formed their own army called the Ulster Volunteer Force. And now, in 1914, their weapons had arrived.

But four months later, World War I broke out. Many thousands of Irishmen, both Catholic and Protestant, joined the British army to fight overseas. For the moment, Home Rule had to wait.

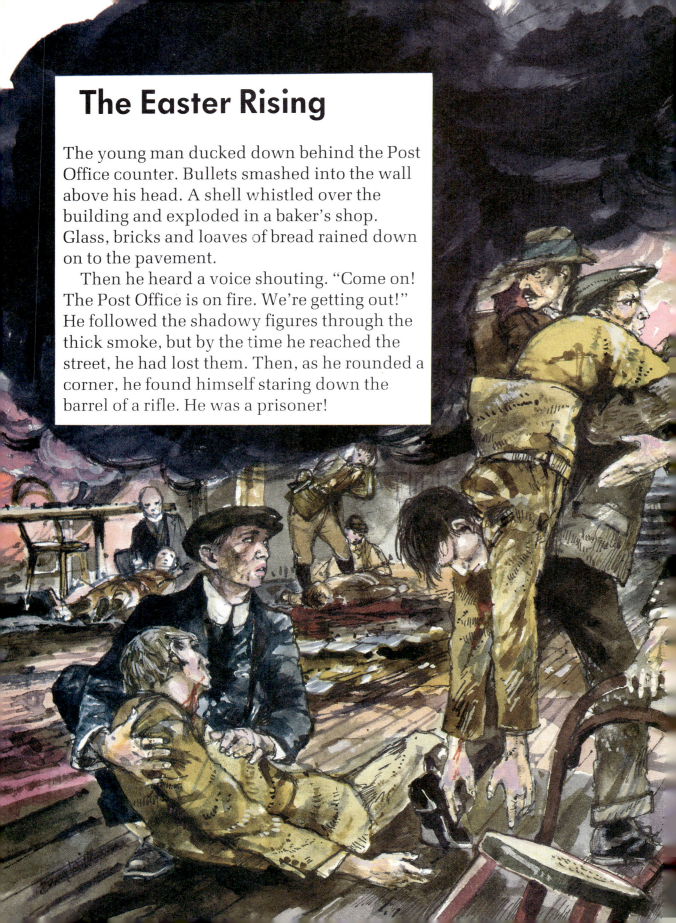

The Easter Rising

The young man ducked down behind the Post Office counter. Bullets smashed into the wall above his head. A shell whistled over the building and exploded in a baker's shop. Glass, bricks and loaves of bread rained down on to the pavement.

Then he heard a voice shouting. "Come on! The Post Office is on fire. We're getting out!" He followed the shadowy figures through the thick smoke, but by the time he reached the street, he had lost them. Then, as he rounded a corner, he found himself staring down the barrel of a rifle. He was a prisoner!

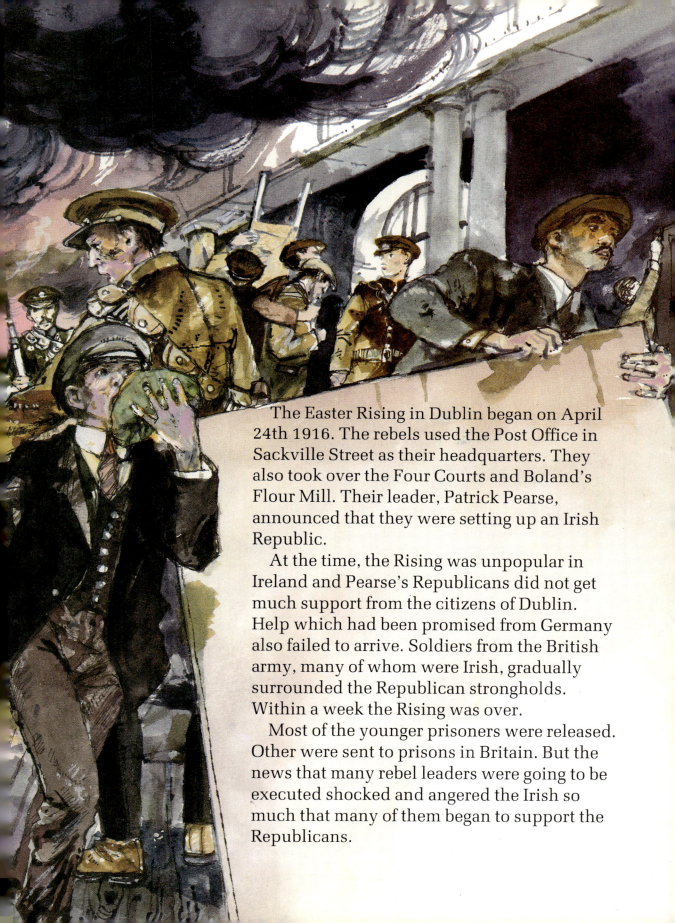

The Easter Rising in Dublin began on April 24th 1916. The rebels used the Post Office in Sackville Street as their headquarters. They also took over the Four Courts and Boland's Flour Mill. Their leader, Patrick Pearse, announced that they were setting up an Irish Republic.

At the time, the Rising was unpopular in Ireland and Pearse's Republicans did not get much support from the citizens of Dublin. Help which had been promised from Germany also failed to arrive. Soldiers from the British army, many of whom were Irish, gradually surrounded the Republican strongholds. Within a week the Rising was over.

Most of the younger prisoners were released. Other were sent to prisons in Britain. But the news that many rebel leaders were going to be executed shocked and angered the Irish so much that many of them began to support the Republicans.

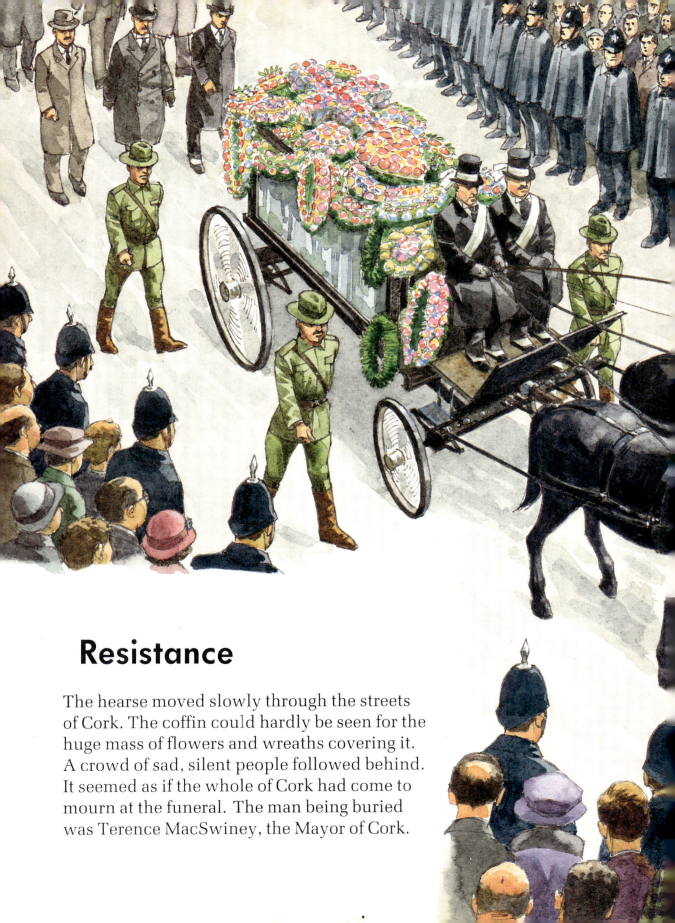

Resistance

The hearse moved slowly through the streets of Cork. The coffin could hardly be seen for the huge mass of flowers and wreaths covering it. A crowd of sad, silent people followed behind. It seemed as if the whole of Cork had come to mourn at the funeral. The man being buried was Terence MacSwiney, the Mayor of Cork.

He had been arrested for distributing leaflets which spoke against the British Government, and had then been sent to prison in Brixton, London.

In prison he went on hunger strike. He refused to eat any food as a protest against the actions of the British in Ireland. He died after seventy-three days, and his body was brought back to Cork for burial.

The death of Terence MacSwiney in 1920 was just one of many tragedies which struck Ireland in the years between 1919 and 1921.

1919, the Irish set up their own Parliament called Dáil Eireann, and declared Ireland a separate state from Britain. The British Government refused to accept this. As a result, the Volunteers, who later became known as the Irish Republican Army or the IRA, began to oppose British rule in Ireland.

As well as sending the British army, the British Government organized a force of special constables to go to Ireland. They were called the Black and Tans, because of the colour of their uniforms. Both sides behaved brutally during the years of protests and fighting that followed as the different groups clashed. The chief newspaper, the Irish Times, reported 'All Ireland streams with blood'.

The Civil War

Darkness was falling as the small group of vehicles swept round the corner. The motor cycle outrider was first to see the obstacles strewn across the road. It was an ambush!

The vehicles screeched to a halt, and at once a hail of bullets swept down on them. After a few minutes, the firing died away. One man stood up slowly and looked around. A rifle cracked and he fell to the ground, dead.

This was how Michael Collins, one of the most famous leaders of the IRA, died one August evening in 1922. He was shot by men who had once been his followers. Why had his friends turned against him?

In 1921 Britain signed a treaty with those Irish who were fighting against them. The treaty said that from now on twenty-six counties in southern Ireland would form a single Irish Free State. The Irish Free State would have its own Parliament, called the Dáil Eireann, but all the members of the Dáil had to take an oath of loyalty to the king of England. The six northern counties would remain a part of Britain.

Many Irish people, including Collins, felt that although they did not get everything they wanted, it was better than nothing. But others felt that they had not won enough

independence. They wanted a republic. The result was a bitter civil war which lasted until 1923.

Collins was Commander of the Irish Free State Army. He led the war against the republicans, many of whom had followed him in the IRA, and so he became their enemy. He was one of many people killed in this war which divided families and brought grief to many homes.

Éamonn de Valera

"Stop!" said the clerk. He sprang to his feet and faced the small group of men entering the Dáil. He pointed to the table on which lay a Bible and a large book. His meaning was clear. No Member of Parliament was allowed into the Dáil until he had signed the book and taken an oath of loyalty to the king of England.

Éamonn de Valera, one of the group, had a problem. He wanted to take his seat in the Irish Parliament. He was prepared to sign his name in the book, but he was not prepared to take an oath of loyalty to the king of England.

De Valera had tried to take his seat in the Dáil before. Each time he had been stopped because he would not take the oath. Everyone held their breath. What would happen this time? Would he be turned away again?

De Valera walked forward to the table, picked up the Bible on which he would swear the oath and handed it to the clerk. He placed his gloves over the words of the oath, so he could say that he had not read them! Then he bent down and signed his name in the large book. He looked hard at the clerk, then moved off to take his seat.

The clerk watched De Valera walk away but made no move to stop him. The oath had not been taken, but the book had been signed. Honour was satisfied.

In this way, in 1927, Éamonn de Valera took his seat in the Dáil. Within a few years he became Prime Minister. Much later, he became president of Ireland and one of the most famous Irishmen who ever lived.

Magnificent men

"Look up there!"

"What is it?"

"What can it be?"

People were running through the streets of Dublin, pointing at a strange object floating high in the air above them. No one had ever seen anything like it.

"It's a balloon!" cried someone in great excitement. "And it's coming down!" Sure enough, the balloon was starting to descend. Shortly afterwards, it landed in the North Strand and the pilot stepped out. Everyone cheered loudly.

On January 19th 1785, Richard Crosbie from Wicklow made a short flight across Dublin in his home-made balloon and so became the first flying Irishman.

Two years later he tried to cross the Irish Sea in a balloon, but was driven back by the wind. It was not until 1817 that an Englishman called William Sadler made the first successful balloon crossing of the Irish Sea.

On December 31st 1909, only seven years after the first aeroplane flight by the Wright brothers, Harry Ferguson made the first powered aeroplane flight in Ireland. His plane flew for a distance of 100 metres, at a height of three metres. In that same year, the first Irish flying display was held at Leopardstown.

Ireland hit the headlines again in 1919, when Alcock and Brown landed their twin-engined Vickers Vimy in a bog at Clifden, County Galway. They had made the first non-stop flight across the Atlantic. The 3,000 kilometre journey had taken them nearly sixteen hours.

Members of a local group, or lodge, carry their banner in the Orange Day Parade.

The Orange Parade

The shrill sound of the pipes and the tap-tapping of the drums can be heard in the distance. "Quick! Come and watch! The Orangemen are here!" The excited children grab their flags and race outside.

The street is already packed with people cheering and waving Union Jacks. The children wriggle through the crowd to get to the front. The first groups are already passing, their orange sashes bright against their dark suits. Overhead, banners flap lazily. Maces flash in the sun as they twirl high in the air.

It is July 12th in Belfast. Members of the Orange Order are taking part in a great parade. They are marching through Belfast to a rally at the 'Field' at Finaghy. They do this every year to celebrate the victory of the Protestant King William III at the Battle of the Boyne in 1689.

The Orange Order began in the 1790s. Today, it has become very powerful. No Government in Northern Ireland could last for long without the support of the Orangemen. In fact, the Order's official title is the Loyal Orange Institution.

Orangemen are organized into local groups called Lodges. On parade, they wear decorations such as orange sashes or orange lilies. Most Orangemen live in Northern Ireland, but there are lodges in England, the Republic of Ireland, Scotland and other countries.

Orangemen wear decorations such as orange sashes and badges. These show to which lodge and church the members belong.

Farming today

Farming has always been one of the most important industries in Ireland. Traditional farming on small plots of land lasted until the beginning of this century. Irish farmers often grew only enough to feed themselves and the local community. But nowadays, it is not just the Irish who eat Irish produce. Irish butter, cheese and beef are sent all over Europe.

There have been many changes in farming in the last hundred years. On cattle farms, vets inspect herds regularly and help to wipe out diseases.

Irish farmers also grow sugar beet and wheat as well as potatoes. The old problem of potato blight has been solved by spraying the crop with a chemical called copper sulphate.

The old hand methods of farming have disappeared. Machines such as tractors and combine harvesters help to make the work much easier and quicker. Sugar beet is turned into sugar in modern factories.

Even the land looks different. The fields are much bigger. Peat is mostly cut by giant mechanical turf cutters, and burned in power stations to produce electricity for farms, factories and homes.

Tankers call daily to collect the milk from the milking shed.

Cheeses are left to mature.

Crops are sprayed by
low-flying helicopters.

This huge machine cuts
slabs of peat.

Great names in sport

Mary Peters had tried twice before. In 1964 she had been placed fourth, in 1968 she had been placed ninth. Now it was the Olympic Games of 1972 in Munich. Mary was fighting for a gold medal in the pentathlon. The pentathlon is a competiton which combines five different events. Marks are awarded for positions in each event.

Everything depended upon the 200 metres race. The West German, Heide Rosenthal, came first in that race. But Mary was only 1.12 seconds behind her and this second place earned her the highest overall marks. Her score broke the world pentathlon record and won her a gold medal. But more than that, Mary's spirit and personality captured the hearts of people all over the world.

Mary Peters clears the bar.

Stephen Roche glides round a bend to pass an opponent.

Ireland has also produced many world-class footballers. Liam Brady's skill is as well-known in Italy as it is in Ireland. Liam has spent many years playing for great Italian football teams, such as Juventus.

Stephen Roche is one of the world's greatest cyclists. In 1987, he became world champion. His name is known throughout Europe, where he is admired and respected. At home he is a national hero.

Barry McGuigan has also shown Ireland some spectacular action. His bravery and determination made him flyweight boxing champion of the world. And his sportsmanship brought all of Ireland together in support of him.

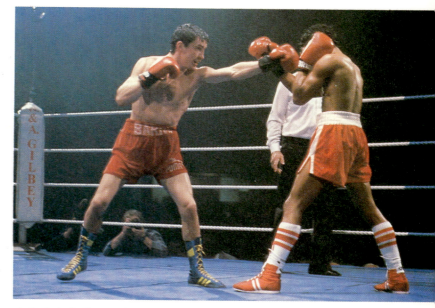

A left jab from Barry McGuigan does its job.

Some sports like hurling and Gaelic football are very specially Irish. The Gaelic Athletic Association was formed to encourage these and other Irish sports. Great players such as the hurler Nicky English are real favourites.

A defender is turned round by Liam Brady.

Nicky English moves forward skilfully.

An Aer Lingus Boeing 737.

Modern Ireland

The Aer Lingus jet touches down at Cork
Airport. Soon the passengers are moving
through the customs hall.

The development of Ireland's transport
system has helped to bring visitors from all
over the world. In 1936, the Irish national
airline, Aer Lingus, was set up. In 1958,
passenger flights to America began. Aer Lingus
is now a major European airline, carrying
passengers all over Europe and North America.

Tourism is also important. Many people
visit Ireland each year to explore its beautiful
scenery and historic landmarks. Flying into
Ireland, the traveller immediately understands
why this island is called the 'Emerald Isle'.
Much of the countryside is still farmland — a
patchwork of parkland and fields, dotted here
and there with small villages and fed by a
wealth of endless rivers and streams.

Modern ways of making cloth in Ireland.

In Northern Ireland, cloth factories which once only produced linen now make man-made fibres. Many other things such as ships and aeroplanes are built in Northern Ireland.

On January 1st 1973, Ireland became a member of the European Economic Community, or EEC. The government provided money to bring foreign industry to the country. Huge industrial estates have sprung up around the big cities of Dublin, Cork and Limerick.

An oil platform.

Storing petroleum.

Special words

ard ri   High king.

curragh   Traditional light skin-covered boats used today by Donegal fishermen.

deilg   A Celtic brooch used to fasten a cloak.

Fenians   A secret society formed during the 1860's to overthrow British Rule.

Fianna   A band of independent warriors famous for their heroic deeds.

filid   Learned men or poets of Celtic society.

gall-oglaigh   Scottish mercenaries used by the Gaelic Irish to help fight the Norman troops.

hurling   A traditional Gaelic sport played with a ball and an ash stick called a caman.

Justiciar   An English king's representative in Ireland.

leine   A long Celtic tunic or shirt.

lunula   A necklace shaped like a crescent moon.

Ogham   Ancient Irish writing, formed of straight lines and carved into stone columns.

Ostmen   The name by which the Vikings in Ireland called themselves.

rath   A circular fort surrounded by banks of earth and a ditch.

ri   A king.

torc   A neck piece made of bronze or gold.

tuath   The name given to a Celtic tribe.

Uillean pipes   A traditional pipe instrument used to accompany dancing.

Index

This index is an alphabetical list of the important words and topics in this book.

When you are looking for a special piece of information, you can look for the word in the list and it will tell you which pages to look at.

Acknowledgement

The publishers of **Childcraft** gratefully acknowledge the following artists, photographers, publishers, agencies and corporations for illustrations used in this volume. All illustrations are the exclusive property of the publishers of **Childcraft** unless names are marked with an asterisk *.

Cover	Terry Thomas (Specs Art Agency)
6–7	Charles Front
8–9	Ray Mutimer (Associated Freelance Artists Ltd)
10–11	Mark Peppé (B. L. Kearley Ltd)
12–13	Donald Harley (B. L. Kearley Ltd)
14–15	Gillian Hunt (Specs Art Agency)
16–17	Terry Thomas (Specs Art Agency)
18–19	Donald Harley (B. L. Kearley Ltd)
20–21	Roger Wade Walker (Specs Art Agency)
22–23	Mark Peppé (B. L. Kearley Ltd)
24–25	Roger Wade Walker (Specs Art Agency)
26–27	Ray Mutimer (Associated Freelance Artists Ltd)
28–29	Mark Peppé (B. L. Kearley Ltd)
30–31	Charles Front; Nicholas Devore (Bruce Coleman Limited*)
32–33	Stephen Conlin (Associated Freelance Artists Ltd); Ken Andrew*
34–35	The Board of Trinity College, Dublin*; National Museum of Ireland*; Office of Public Works, Dublin*
36–37	Barry Wilkinson (B. L. Kearley Ltd)
38–39	Roger Wade Walker (Specs Art Agency)
40–41	Stephen Conlin (Associated Freelance Artists Ltd)
42–43	Terry Thomas (Specs Art Agency)
44–45	Ray Mutimer (Associated Freelance Artists Ltd)
46–47	Gillian Hunt (Specs Art Agency)
48–49	Nigel Alexander (Specs Art Agency)
50–51	Michael Strand (B. L. Kearley Ltd)
52–53	Charles Front
54–55	Ray Mutimer (Associated Freelance Artists Ltd)
56–57	Gillian Hunt (Specs Art Agency)
58–61	Roger Wade Walker (Specs Art Agency)